# the gluten-free baker

# the gluten-free baker

delicious baked treats for the gluten intolerant

Hannah Miles
photography by William Reavell

rps
LONDON • NEW YORK

**Dedication**
For my friend Lucy, the inspiration for this book.

**Senior Designer** Megan Smith
**Senior Commissioning Editor** Julia Charles
**Production** Gordana Simakovic
**Art Director** Leslie Harrington
**Publishing Director** Alison Starling

**Prop Stylist** Liz Belton
**Food Stylist** Joss Herd
**Indexer** Hilary Bird

First published in 2011 by Ryland Peters & Small
20–21 Jockey's Fields, London WC1R 4BW
and
Ryland Peters & Small Inc.
519 Broadway, 5th Floor
New York, NY10012
www.rylandpeters.com

10 9 8 7 6 5



ISBN: 978-1-84975-137-7



A CIP record for this book is available from the British Library.
US Library of Congress cataloguing-in-publication data has been applied for.

Printed and bound in China

**Author's acknowledgements**
A huge thank you to Ryland Peters & Small for publishing this book (a very special project that I hope inspires people to bake) – in particular to my editor Julia Charles, a lovely friend to work with; Megan Smith for her beautiful book design; Joss Herd for her inspirational food styling; and to William Reavell for his stunning photography. Much love to David, Christine, Lucy, Jennifer, Maren, Elke, Jess and Susan for their kind contributions and to Sacha for his love and support whilst writing this book.

A very special thank you goes to Amy Peterson of **Coeliac UK** for her help and guidance – Coeliac UK is a leading charity working for people living with coeliac disease and dermatitis herpetiformis. Visit them at www.coeliac.org.uk or call the Helpline on 0845 305 2060 for information and support. In the US visit www.celiac.org or www.celiac.com for information, advice and support.

# contents

# Introduction

Several years ago my very good friend Lucy was diagnosed as having a gluten intolerance. The time before she was diagnosed was very frightening as the doctors couldn't seem to find out what was making her so ill. She was in pain a lot of the time, completely lacking in energy and ended up in hospital on several occasions. When she was eventually diagnosed as having a gluten intolerance, it seemed incredible that something as simple as wheat could have made her so poorly. Having got over the initial relief that her illness was not life threatening, the next hurdle was a change of diet, which didn't prove as easy as Lucy had hoped. Whilst there are quite a few gluten-free products available in supermarkets, not all of them are particularly palatable. Lucy found that items were often powdery and had a chemical taste and just weren't adequate substitutes for the cakes, breads and pastry that she missed. Eating out was also difficult as not everywhere catered for those on gluten-free diets. Those that said they did would invariably offer coconut macaroons as the only choice. When we tried a 'gluten-free afternoon tea' in a top London hotel our expectations were high, so you can imagine our disappointment when we cut into the gluten-free scones and they literally crumbled to dust. By this time I had realized that there had to be a better solution to easy gluten-free baking.

I read a lot of books on gluten-free cooking to try and help Lucy find some new recipes. These seemed to require endless combining of different flours and a lengthy list of non-storecupboard ingredients. There seemed to be no clear explanation of which flour to use when and in what quantities. All in all it was very intimidating even for someone who bakes as much as I do. What I wanted was some good basic recipes that used ingredients that I was familiar with, gluten-free plain and self-raising flours, ground nuts, polenta, desiccated coconut and such like. Ready-combined flours seemed the simplest solution and avoided the need for combining many different types of gluten-free flour – such as tapioca, potato and rice – as they have already been combined by the manufacturers in what I imagine must be the best possible combination following rigorous testing. Using these ready-blended flours lets you bake as you would with regular flour and achieve excellent results. Keep two or three bags in the kitchen storecupboard and you can bake perfect gluten-free cakes, breads and pastry whenever needed. It is then just a question of understanding the characteristics of the particular gluten-free flours you are using, and adding other ingredients to provide the extra moisture needed and plenty of flavour.

One thing I have noticed about most people who suffer from a gluten intolerance is that they don't want to stand out as different from other people – they just want to be served something 'normal' and not be made to feel like they are causing inconvenience. The aim of this book is therefore simple: to make things that taste so good that you would never know they were gluten-free. You can serve these recipes to the whole family and all of your friends and no one will notice the difference. It also means you will avoid the need to bake two different recipes for the one occasion!

This book aims to provide delicious alternatives to those favourite recipes that people suffering from coeliac disease or gluten intolerance miss the most – pastries, breads and cakes – simple home-baking that when you are first diagnosed seem like an impossibility. With a little know-how and some simple ingredients, this book will return you to baking.

Fortunately, food manufacturers, restaurants and shops are now offering a more comprehensive range of gluten-free products, reflecting the increased understanding and recognition of gluten intolerance, but there are few things nicer than tucking into something you have baked yourself. I hope that this book will give you the tools to realize that being unable to eat gluten doesn't mean you can't be a home baker and rustle up delicious warm baked treats for yourself and others. So don your apron, get out your whisk and start baking today!

## What is Coeliac Disease?

Coeliac disease is an auto-immune disease, which affect the intestines, leading to poor absorption of gluten. Symptoms of coeliac disease can leave those affected feeling very unwell and lacking in energy, as well as having an upset stomach and other symptoms. There is currently no cure for the condition but it can be managed well with a change in diet. It is important that medical advice is taken by anyone who feels they might be experiencing a sensitivity to gluten, to ascertain whether they are a coeliac or are experiencing an allergic reaction to gluten and/or wheat. Each person's symptoms are unique – some people will be able to eat some ingredients that cause problems for others. Testing is available and it is important to take steps to understand what is safe for you to eat. For my friend Lucy, this was a steep learning curve but within a few months she knew which brands of chocolate, poppadoms and stock cubes didn't contain gluten and were safe for her to enjoy Sometimes coeliac disease is also coupled with other allergies and you may find that some other products, which are gluten-free, also make you unwell. With time and experience you will have a clear understanding of your own limitations.

Gluten is present in varying levels in wheat, barley and rye cereals and also sometimes in oats, although this is thought most likely caused by cross-contamination with other cereals. Some sensitive to gluten can eat oats and as these are a good staple ingredient in baking, some of the recipes in this book use them but always make sure you buy brands labelled 'gluten-free' to be safe. You should always check, however, whether the person you are baking for is intolerant to oats.

## Managing a Gluten-free Diet

Whilst it is easy to avoid products that obviously contain wheat and gluten – bread, cakes, pasta – there are a variety of products that contain traces of gluten, some of which are not obvious. It is not always easy to avoid such pitfalls and it is therefore essential to carefully check the ingredients list on product packaging or refer to the manufacturer to ensure that products are gluten-free. At the outset of a gluten-free diet you may find it helps to keep a food diary to record what you eat as this can help to identify problem foods that have made you ill. Some brands of a type of product may be gluten-free whereas others may not – very careful reading of ingredients labels is always essential. Nowadays many products are labelled as 'gluten-free', which makes life much easier.

All forms of wheat, barley, rye and spelt must be avoided. This means that regular flours and breads are out, as well as wheat-based products, such as beer and pasta. Gluten is also commonly used by food manufacturers in a wide variety of food preparation and can be found in ready-meals and pre-produced food. A small trace of wheat used as a thickener in a sauce may make you really unwell but checking the labelling will help you to spot unsafe ingredients. Products that are coated in breadcrumbs are also not suitable for people with gluten intolerance.

You need to be extra vigilant at all stages of cooking. It is so easy to take a packet from the kitchen cupboard and add to a recipe without checking whether the item contains gluten – I have found myself doing this on occasion and have just stopped myself in time. I once made stock from chicken bones of a roast chicken, but the chicken had contained a breadcrumb stuffing so there was a good chance that the stock was contaminated with gluten. Luckily I remembered in time before serving to my friend who is a coeliac. With time and practice you will become familiar with which ingredients are safe and which are not. The best advice is just to take a bit of time before you start cooking. Assemble all of your ingredients and check that they are all safe to use before starting to cook.

Some of the less obvious products that contain gluten include:

**Anti-caking agents** – these are used to prevent clumping and sticking together of ingredients during food production and can contain traces of wheat. Anti-caking agents are commonly found in some icing/confectioners' sugars and dried fruits. When using these sugars and dried fruits always check the labels carefully to ensure that they do not contain an anti-caking agent. Powdered fondant icing sugar (which contains glucose) and unrefined icing/confectioners' sugar do not generally contain an anti-caking agent and can be used to make glacé, royal and butter icings/frostings successfully. When selecting dried fruit, choose those brands that are separated using a light coating of oil rather than an anti-caking agent.

**Yeast** – some dried yeasts contain wheat as a bulking agent. For safe gluten-free baking, use either fresh yeast or a gluten-free dried yeast, both of which are stocked by most supermarkets and health food shops.

**Baking powder** – some baking powders contain wheat. Many manufacturers are now using rice flour in place of wheat flour and so gluten-free baking powder is now more commonly available in supermarkets.

**Dried milk powder/non-fat dry milk** – for a while Lucy couldn't understand why she felt ill after eating shop-bought ice cream and chocolate. We discovered that some milk powders/non-fat dry milk are bulked out with wheat. In addition, some coeliacs cannot tolerate white or milk chocolate because lactose interolance is associated with coeliac disease, although it is a temporary condition in the vast majority of people that rectifies itself after a person establishes themselves on a gluten-free diet.

**Malt products** – malted drinks should all be avoided as they are wheat based, but malt extract can usually be tolerated in small amounts, e.g. in breakfast cereals. Malt vinegar is suitable as the protein is removed in the processing.

**Soy sauce and Worcestershire sauce** – these also contain gluten so look out for gluten-free brands.

**Processed meat products** – products such as sausages, salamis and pâtés can contain traces of wheat so always read the labels carefully.

**Sauces, gravy powders, stocks (cubes and liquid) and powdered spices** – these can sometimes be bulked out with wheat products so again always check the labels carefully.

**Instant coffees** – some contain wheat as a bulking agent. Fresh ground coffee, which can be used to make espresso or filter coffee in a machine can be used instead as these generally do not contain any gluten.

**Glacé cherries** – these can contain gluten. Use fresh cherries or preserved cherries as a good substitute in baking, they always taste nicer anyway in my opinion!

**Sour cream** – some processes for making sour cream use wheat so it is important to use a brand that is 'pure' and gluten-free. Checking the manufacturers' website will assist with this.

The above list is not exhaustive but should give you a good idea of just how rigorous you have to be with product checking when you are cooking for someone with a gluten intolerance.

## Gluten-free Baking

The key to successful gluten-free baking is to understand the ingredients and their properties. Gluten gives elasticity to the doughs from which breads and cakes are made. Gluten-free substitutes lack this elasticity and need to be handled slightly differently. The one good thing is that as the doughs are not elastic, bread doughs need no kneading, sparing your arm muscles somewhat! Generally speaking, gluten-free doughs and mixes require a lot more liquid than wheat-based recipes and if there is not enough liquid the items will have a powdery texture and crumble when you cut them. Adding natural yogurt, buttermilk or sour cream to cake mixtures will result in moist cakes. Pastry can be very crumbly without the elasticity of gluten and must be very carefully worked. Adding cheese to savoury pastry or cream cheese to sweet pastry can help bind the dough together. Rather than rolling the pastry out into large sheets that are likely to crumble when lifted, the best method for lining a pastry case is to gently press in small pieces of the pastry dough into the tin/pan until it is lined entirely with a thin layer of pastry.

Some gluten-free flours can have a slightly bitter taste that can spoil the flavour of baked goods. The best way to mask this is to make sure that each recipe is packed full of flavour.

## The Gluten-free Baking Pantry

For successful baking you need to equip yourself with a few basic ingredients. Once you have developed confidence from following these recipes, you can then experiment with other recipes. Below is a list of essential ingredients you will need for baking the recipes from this book.

**Gluten-free blended flours** – there is now a wide variety of gluten-free flours available in supermarkets and wholefood stores and these are the easiest flours to start with. They are ready mixed and are specifically designed to give the best results. In the UK three types are available – plain flour for cookies and pastry, self-raising flour for cakes and some breads, and strong white flour for breads and some pastries. In the US all-purpose flour is available but I've yet to find a self-raising/rising one so have tested the recipes in this book with Bob's Red Mill gluten-free all-purpose baking flour, adding gluten-free baking powder and xanthan gum, which gives a very good result. Whilst you can combine your own mixes of rice, potato and cornflour/cornstarch, it is more convenient to use these ready-mixed flours.
**Buckwheat flour** – contrary to its name, buckwheat does not contain any wheat at all. It is made from the seeds of a flowering plant that is associated with the rhubarb family. The seeds look similar to beechnuts and it is a common misunderstanding that this flour is made from beechnuts. The flour has a strong

taste, which can be quite overpowering and slightly medicinal if used in large quantities. This flour is ideal for pancakes and blinis and can be used in some cakes. (Be aware that a very small number of people experience an allergic reaction to buckwheat so it's always essential to check with the person you are baking for.)

**Chestnut flour** – this is made from ground sweet chestnuts and has a delicious smoky flavour. Due to this smokiness, however, it is only really suitable for savoury recipes.

**Gram flour** – this is made from ground chickpeas and is often used in Indian cookery. It can be used to make pakora and bhajis and also various Indian flatbreads. Most poppadoms are made with gram flour but it is important to check that it has not been combined with wheat flour. Italian *farina di ceci* is a similar product and can be substituted.

**Coconut flour** – this is made from dried coconut flesh, which has been ground to a fine powder. You can make your own by grinding desiccated coconut to a fine powder in a food processor and then sifting it, although if your desiccated coconut is sweetened you will need to reduce the sugar in the recipe and check that the desiccated coconut does not contain any wheat as an anti-caking agent or coating (for more information see page 9).

**Cornflour/cornstarch** – this is made from finely ground grains of corn. It is an excellent thickener and can be used in sauces.

**Polenta/cornmeal** – this is a useful staple of gluten-free baking. Coarse grains can be cooked in water to a thick paste and added to cakes and breads to give a lovely golden colour, moist texture and rich flavour. Fine meal is more like flour in texture and can be used in breads and muffins.

**Almond meal and ground almonds** – almond meal is a coarse ground flour which contains the skin of the whole almonds. It is therefore darker in texture than ground almonds and is ideal in cookies and cakes. Ground almonds are one of the most common ingredients in this book as they make cakes very moist and do not have a strong flavour so can carry other flavours well. You can make you own ground almonds or almond meal by blitzing whole or skinned almonds in a food processor. When buying ready ground almonds check the ingredients as some cheap varieties include breadcrumbs as a bulking agent (and therefore gluten).

**Nuts** – a lot of the recipes in this book use other ground nuts, such as pecans, walnuts and hazelnuts. They are an ideal replacement for flour – they create a moist texture and add delicious flavour. If you do not have the nut called for in the recipe you can

generally substitute another nut in its place. By grinding the nuts in a food processor until very fine then combining them with a small amount of gluten-free flour they make an ideal substitute.
**Gluten-free baking powder** – this is an essential raising/rising agent and is used to make cakes and breads rise during baking.
**Xanthan gum** – this is used in gluten-free baking to bind, thicken and stabilize ingredients and is ideal for use in doughs, pastry and breads. It's made by fermenting corn sugar with a microbial bacteria and is used extensively in the food industry.
**Extra virgin coconut oil** – this is usually sold in jars in a set form and adds a delicious coconut flavour to recipes.
**Flavouring agents** – vanilla and almond extracts are ideal for masking the sometimes mildly unpleasant 'flavour' of gluten-free flours. Always check the labelling to ensure that flavourings are gluten-free.
**Dairy ingredients** – these are essential for moist, non-crumbly cakes – in this book the recipes use buttermilk, plain yogurt and sour cream. Again it is essential to check the product labels as some creams may contain traces of gluten. If you prefer you can make your own sour cream by adding the juice of a lemon to 300 ml/1¼ cups double/heavy cream. If you do not have the liquid ingredient called for in the recipe you can easily substitute – for example if you do not have buttermilk available mix together half milk and half plain yogurt to the same quantity of buttermilk. The results will be equally delicious.
**Syrups and honeys** – pure maple syrup, golden/light corn syrup, treacle and honey are all gluten-free and are delicious sweeteners in baking recipes.
**Oats** – not all people who are intolerant to gluten are able to eat oats. If in doubt do not use them. However there are many people who are intolerant to gluten who are able to eat oats but make sure you choose brands labelled gluten-free to be safe.
**Eggs** – eggs do not contain gluten and are used in most of the recipes in this book. By separating the eggs and whisking the egg whites separately and folding into a cake batter, you can add additional air to your cakes, making them light and delicious.
**Butter and fats** – some margarines may contain gluten so it is best to use good-quality unsalted butter in all recipes to remain gluten-free.
**Alcohols** – this can be a slightly confusing area for those who are gluten-intolerant. Beer is made with hops and so must be avoided. Some brands of whiskey (and cream-based whiskey liqueurs) may contain gluten from the caramel colouring which is added, although pure whiskey does not contain gluten. Before using any alcohol check with the manufacturer to ascertain whether it is gluten-free.

## Avoiding Contamination

One key requirement of successful gluten-free baking is to avoid cross-contamination. If you have a member of the family who is intolerant to gluten, the best solution is to remove all products containing gluten from the house. Whilst this is the most effective way to avoid the risk of cross contamination, I recognize that this is not always practical. Where total removal is not possible, the best advice is to keep gluten-free products in sealed containers in a separate place away from products containing gluten. Label everything clearly so that there can be no confusion as to what is gluten-free.

If you have been baking with regular flour, small particles will have been released into the air during cooking can land on cooking equipment, surfaces and even kitchen towels and leave traces of gluten. It is therefore important to wipe down all equipment,

surfaces and utensils thoroughly and use clean cloths and aprons. It takes a surprisingly small amount of exposure to gluten to make someone ill.

Cross-contamination is also possible through using kitchen appliances and equipment, such as toasters, baking sheets and wire racks. Silicone sleeves (Toastabags) can be used to shield toasters from gluten contamination or, if possible, have a separate toaster and other similar appliances just for gluten-free products. Also consider investing in some silicon mats that you can set aside just for gluten-free baking. It is also important to avoid putting knives and spoons that have been exposed to gluten into butters, spreads and jams/jellies as these can also cause contamination. If it is practical have separate tubs and jars clearly labelled as 'gluten-free'. Where possible store these away from products that may contain traces of gluten.

## Where to Go for Advice

If you believe that you may have a gluten intolerance or coeliac disease, it is essential to seek professional medical advice. Once you have been diagnosed with either, there are many sources of information available to you. The Coeliac Societies in the UK and USA are able to provide a large amount of advice and support (see page 4). Local support groups can also offer guidance on managing day-to-day life without gluten. In addition, there are a wide variety of books on this subject and some fantastic resources are available on-line offering a wealth of information. Particularly useful are the forums where coeliacs can communicate with each other and share advice on all aspects of living and enjoying a gluten-free lifestyle.

# cookies, brownies & bars

These giant chocolate chip cookies will put a smile on everyone's face. Delicious with a glass of ice-cold milk, packed full of dark and white chocolate, they are a perfect home-coming treat. It is important that the chocolate you use does not contain milk powder as this can contains gluten so check the labels carefully. Gluten-free white chocolate buttons are available in most larger supermarkets.

# chocolate chip cookies

**125 g/1 stick plus 1 tablespoon unsalted butter, softened**
**125 g/⅔ cup caster/granulated sugar**
**125 g/½ cup dark soft brown sugar**
**150 g/1 cup plus 2 tablespoons gluten-free plain/all-purpose baking flour**
**1 teaspoon bicarbonate of soda/baking soda**
**100 g/1 cup ground almonds**
**1 egg, beaten**
**60 ml/¼ cup buttermilk**
**100 g/3½ oz dark chocolate, chopped**
**100 g/3½ oz white chocolate buttons**

*2 baking sheets, greased and lined*

Makes about 20 cookies

Preheat the oven to 180°C (350°F) Gas 4.

Put the butter and both sugars in a mixing bowl and cream together. Add the flour, bicarbonate of soda/baking soda, ground almonds, egg and buttermilk and whisk well until everything is incorporated. Mix in the dark chocolate and white chocolate buttons with a wooden spoon.

Put 20 tablespoonfuls of the mixture on the prepared baking sheets, leaving a gap between each one as the cookies will spread during baking. (You may need to bake in batches depending on the size of your baking sheets.)

Bake in the preheated oven for about 10–12 minutes, until the cookies are golden brown. Leave to cool on the baking sheets for a few minutes then transfer to a wire rack to cool completely.

These cookies will keep for up to 5 days if stored in an airtight container.

MADE IN ENGLAND BY
A. S WILKIN LTD.
CREMONA PARK, NEWCASTLE UPON TYNE

These oat and coconut cookies are delicious and have a crisp buttery texture – perfect for an afternoon teatime treat. I prefer to make these cookies whilst the mixture is still warm from heating the syrup as this causes the cookies to spread out thinly and gives a crisp buttery texture. If you prefer a chewier cookie, let the mixture go cold and place mounds of the dough on the baking sheet, as the cookies will spread out less this way. Please bear in mind that not all people with gluten or wheat intolerance can eat oats but gluten-free oats are now available so these should always be used.

# oat & coconut cookies

**150 g/1 stick plus 2 tablespoons butter**
**3 generous tablespoons golden/light corn syrup**
**170 g/1 cup gluten-free porridge/rolled oats**
**85 g/1 generous cup long soft shredded coconut**
**60 g/1 scant cup flaked coconut**
**115 g/½ cup plus 1 tablespoon caster/ granulated sugar**
**115 g gluten-free self-raising flour OR 1 scant cup gluten-free all-purpose baking flour plus 1 teaspoon baking powder and ¼ teaspoon xanthan gum**

*2 baking sheets, greased and lined*

Makes about 24 cookies

Preheat the oven to 180°C (350°F) Gas 4.

Put the butter and syrup in a small saucepan and melt over gentle heat. Put the oats, both coconuts, sugar and flour in a mixing bowl. Pour the melted butter mixture over the dry ingredients and mix well with a wooden spoon, until everything is incorporated.

Put 24 tablespoonfuls of the mixture on the prepared baking sheets, a distance apart as they will spread during baking. (You may need to bake in batches depending on the size of your baking sheets.)

Bake in the preheated oven for 10–15 minutes, until the cookies are golden brown. Watch closely towards the end of cooking as they can turn brown very quickly. Leave to cool on the baking sheets.

These cookies will keep for up to 5 days if stored in an airtight container.

Ginger cookies are perfect on a cold day. Warming pieces of ginger and tangy lime always soothe away life's troubles. If you prefer, you can replace the lime zest with orange zest and a pinch of cinnamon for a more festive feel. These cookies store well in an airtight tin and can be frozen on the day they are made.

# ginger cookies

**160 g gluten-free self-raising flour OR 1⅓ cups gluten-free all-purpose baking flour plus 1½ teaspoons baking powder and ¾ teaspoon xanthan gum**
**1 teaspoon bicarbonate of soda/baking soda**
**180 g/2 cups ground almonds**
**180 g/1 cup caster/granulated sugar**
**2 teaspoons ground ginger**
**finely grated zest of 2 limes**
**125 g/1 stick plus 1 tablespoon butter**
**6 pieces of stem ginger in syrup, finely chopped plus 3 tablespoons ginger syrup from the jar**

*2 baking sheets, greased and lined*

Makes about 18 cookies

Preheat the oven to 180°C (350°F) Gas 4.

Put the flour, bicarbonate of soda/baking soda, ground almonds, caster sugar, ground ginger and lime zest in a mixing bowl and mix together. Put the butter and ginger syrup in a small saucepan and heat gently until the butter has melted. Let cool slightly and then stir into the dry ingredients, along with the chopped ginger. Put about 18 tablespoonfuls of the mixture on the prepared baking sheets, leaving a gap between each as the cookies will spread during cooking. (You may need to bake in batches depending on the size of your baking sheets.)

Bake in the preheated oven for about 12–15 minutes, until the cookies are golden brown. Leave to cool on the baking sheets for a few minutes then transfer to a wire rack with a spatula to cool.

These cookies will keep for up to 5 days if stored in an airtight container.

Marzipan is one of life's little luxuries. It gives these cookies a heady almond flavour and makes them delicately chewy. Flavoured with cinnamon and spices, these stars are delicious served with warm mulled wine for a festive treat.

# almond stars

**200 g/⅔ cup gluten-free marzipan**
**90 g/6 tablespoons butter, softened**
**60 g gluten-free self-raising flour OR ½ cup gluten-free all-purpose baking flour plus ½ teaspoon baking powder and ⅛ teaspoon xanthan gum**
**120 g/1¼ cups ground almonds**
**30 g/2 tablespoons almond meal**
**1 teaspoon vanilla extract**
**1 teaspoon ground cinnamon**
**1 teaspoon mixed spice/apple pie spice**

***For the icing***
**1 egg white**
**100 g/¾ cup powdered fondant icing sugar**

*a 5-cm/2-in star-shaped cookie cutter*

*2 baking sheets, greased and lined*

Makes about 35 cookies

Preheat the oven to 180°C (350°F) Gas 4.

Break the marzipan into small pieces and put it in a bowl with the butter. Cream together until the mixture is paste-like. Sift in the flour and add the ground almonds, almond meal, vanilla extract and spices and beat to a smooth, soft dough. The mixture should be very soft but not sticky so add a little more flour if needed.

Dust a work surface with flour. Roll out the dough to a 1-cm/½-in thickness using a rolling pin. Use the cutter to stamp out 35 stars. Arrange the stars on the baking sheets a small distance apart as they will spread a little during baking. Bake in the preheated oven for 10–15 minutes, until golden brown. Remove from the oven and leave to cool slightly on the baking sheet.

To ice, whisk the egg white to stiff peaks and sift in the powdered fondant icing sugar. Fold together until you have a smooth icing. Use a pastry brush to coat the tops of the cookies whilst they are still warm. Leave to set for 5 minutes then apply a second coat of icing. Allow the icing to set completely before serving.

These cookies will keep for up to 2 weeks if stored in an airtight container.

I first discovered the delights of macarons when I was given a box from the chic Parisian tearoom Ladurée. I was transfixed by these brightly coloured dainty treats, nestled between layers of tissue paper. These are my own version of a French classic.

# walnut & cinnamon macarons

**60 g/generous ½ cup ground almonds**
**60 g/½ cup walnut pieces**
**25 g/1 generous tablespoon dark soft brown sugar**
**2 teaspoons ground cinnamon**
**150 g/1 cup powdered fondant icing sugar**
**3 egg whites (about 90 g/3¼ oz.)**
**75 g/⅓ cup caster/superfine sugar**
**a few drops of orange food colouring**

***For the filling***
**100 g/1 cup walnut pieces**
**50 g/3½ tablespoons butter**
**200 g/1½ cups icing/confectioners' sugar**
**2 tablespoons double/heavy cream**

*2 piping bags, both fitted with large round nozzles/tips*

*a baking sheet, lined*

Makes 12 macarons

Put the ground almonds, walnuts, brown sugar, cinnamon and fondant icing sugar in a food processor and blitz to a very fine powder. Sift into a mixing bowl and return any pieces that do not pass through the sieve/strainer to the blender, blitz, then sift again.

Whisk the egg whites to stiff peaks, adding the caster/superfine sugar a spoonful at a time, until the meringue is smooth and glossy. Use a spatula to fold in the walnut mixture a third at a time, along with a few drops of food colouring. It needs to be folded until it is soft enough to just not hold a peak. Drop a little onto a plate and if it folds to a smooth surface it is ready. If it holds a peak then you need to fold it a few further times. If you fold it too much it will be too runny and the macarons will not retain their shape.

Spoon the mixture into one of the piping bags. Pipe 6-cm/2½-in rounds onto the baking sheet a small distance apart. Leave to set on the baking sheets for 1 hour so that the surface of the macarons forms a skin.

Preheat the oven to 170°C (325°F) Gas 3. Bake in the preheated oven for 15–20 minutes, until firm. Leave to cool on the baking sheets.

Meanwhile make the filling. Blitz the walnuts in a food processor until very finely chopped. Add the butter and blend again. Transfer to a mixing bowl with the icing/confectioners' sugar and cream and whisk together until light. Spoon the filling into the second piping bag and pipe a swirl onto half of the cooled macarons. Top each with a second macaron and serve.

These macarons will keep for up to 3 days if stored in an airtight container.

These crisp almond nougatines are perfect with a cup of coffee – the heady scent of almond extract and rich dark chocolate make these the perfect pick-me-up!

# almond & chocolate nougatines

**3 egg whites**
**115 g/½ cup plus 1 tablespoon caster/superfine sugar**
**85 g/generous ¾ cup ground almonds**
**1 teaspoon almond extract**
**30 g gluten-free self-raising flour OR ¼ cup gluten-free all-purpose baking flour plus ¼ teaspoon baking powder**

***To decorate***
**100 g/3½ oz dark chocolate (70% cocoa solids), melted**

*a baking sheet, greased and lined*

*a piping bag, fitted with a large round nozzle/tip*

Makes 16 nougatines

Preheat the oven to 150°C (300°F) Gas 2.

Put the egg whites in a large grease-free bowl and use a handheld electric mixer to whisk until stiff peaks form. Add the sugar a spoonful at a time, whisking after each addition.

Use a spatula to gently fold in the ground almonds, almond extract and flour.

Spoon the mixture into the piping bag and pipe 5-cm/2-in rounds onto the prepared baking sheet a small distance apart. Bake in the preheated oven for 1½–2 hours, until the nougatines are crisp.

Use a teaspoon or the tines of a fork to drizzle each one with a little melted chocolate and allow to set before serving.

These nougatines will keep for up to 1 week if stored in an airtight container.

Two delicious teatime treats – the flapjack and the brownie – are combined in this tempting recipe. The base is packed with coconut and pecans and the brownie rich with dark chocolate. If you are not able to find hazelnut flour, you can substitute gluten-free plain/all-purpose baking flour.

# flapjack pecan brownies

***For the flapjack base***
**125 g/1 stick plus 1 tablespoon butter**
**100 g/½ cup caster/granulated sugar**
**100 g/1 scant cup desiccated coconut**
**100 g/1 cup shelled pecans, finely chopped**

***For the brownie topping***
**125 g/1 stick plus 1 tablespoon butter**
**200 g/7 oz dark chocolate (70% cocoa solids)**
**125 g/⅔ cup caster/granulated sugar**
**125 g/½ cup plus 1 tablespoon dark soft brown sugar**
**3 eggs**
**1 teaspoon vanilla extract**
**100 g/1 cup hazelnut flour**

*a 33 x 23-cm/13 x 9-in baking tin/pan, greased and base-lined*

Makes 20 brownies

Preheat the oven to 190°C (375°F) Gas 5.

To make the flapjack base, put the butter in a saucepan and melt over low heat. Stir in the sugar, coconut and pecans. Mix well so that everything is coated in butter and sugar. Spoon the mixture into the prepared tin/pan and press down evenly with the back of a spoon.

To make the brownie topping, melt the butter and chocolate in a heatproof bowl set over a pan of simmering water. Remove the bowl from the heat and set aside to cool. Put both the sugars, eggs and vanilla extract in a mixing bowl and whisk until the mixture is very light and has doubled in size. Whilst still whisking, slowly pour in the cooled chocolate and butter mixture.

Fold in the hazelnut flour and pour the mixture into the prepared tin/pan. Bake in the preheated oven for about 30–40 minutes, until the topping has formed a crust and a knife inserted in the middle of the brownie comes out clean. Let cool before cutting into squares to serve.

These brownies will keep for up to 5 days if stored in an airtight container.

These are moist, crumbly brownies that quite literally melt in the mouth. Walnuts are ground finely and used in place of flour, which is what gives the brownies such a wonderfully nutty flavour.

# white chocolate & walnut brownies

**250 g/2 sticks plus 2 tablespoons butter**
**300 g/10½ oz dark chocolate (70% cocoa solids)**
**300 g/1½ cups plus 1 tablespoon caster/ granulated sugar**
**200 g/1½ cups dark soft brown sugar**
**5 large eggs**
**1 teaspoon vanilla extract**
**100 g gluten-free self-raising flour OR generous ¾ cup gluten-free all-purpose baking flour plus 1 teaspoon baking powder and ½ teaspoon xanthan gum**
**200 g/2 cups shelled walnuts, finely ground**
**150 g/1 cup white chocolate buttons**

*a 33 x 23-cm/13 x 9-in baking tin/pan, greased and base-lined*

Makes 20 brownies

Preheat the oven to 190°C (375°F) Gas 5.

Melt the butter and dark chocolate in a heatproof bowl set over a pan of simmering water or in a microwave proof bowl in the microwave on high power for 1 minute and stir to ensure there are no lumps. Set aside to cool.

Whisk the caster/granulated sugar and dark brown sugar with the eggs and vanilla extract until the mixture is very light and has doubled in size. Whilst still whisking, slowly pour in the melted chocolate and butter mixture. Fold in the flour and ground walnuts, then pour the mixture into the prepared tin/pan. Sprinkle over the chocolate buttons (which should sink into the mixture) ensuring that they are evenly distributed.

Bake in the preheated oven for about 30–40 minutes, until the brownies have formed a crust and a knife inserted into the middle of the tin/pan comes out clean with no cake batter on it. Allow to cool before cutting into squares.

These brownies will keep for up to 5 days if stored in an airtight container.

Caramel or millionaire's shortbread is always popular – a buttery cookie base with a layer of rich, gooey caramel topped with milk/semisweet chocolate. You can replace the milk chocolate topping with dark or white gluten-free chocolate if you prefer and decorate with gluten-free sprinkles for a pretty party effect.

# caramel shortbread

***For the shortbread base***

**115 g/1 stick butter, softened**

**60 g/⅓ cup caster/granulated sugar**

**85 g gluten-free self-raising flour OR ¾ cup gluten-free all-purpose baking flour plus 1 teaspoon baking powder and ⅛ teaspoon xanthan gum**

**85 g/1 cup ground almonds**

***For the caramel layer***

**60 g/⅓ cup caster/granulated sugar**

**60 g/½ stick butter**

**300 g/1 cup condensed milk**

**1 teaspoon vanilla extract**

***For the chocolate topping***

**150 g/5½ oz milk/semisweet chocolate**

*a 20-cm/8-in square baking tin/pan, greased and lined (base and sides)*

Makes 16 shortbreads

Preheat the oven to 180°C (350°F) Gas 4.

To make the shortbread base, put the butter and sugar in a mixing bowl and cream together. Sift in the flour then add the almonds and bring the mixture together with your hands to form a soft dough. Press into the prepared tin/pan and prick all over with a fork. Bake in the preheated oven for 15–20 minutes, until the shortbread is golden brown. Let cool in the tin/pan.

Put the sugar, butter, condensed milk and vanilla extract in a small saucepan and warm over gentle heat until the butter has melted and the sugar dissolved. Bring to the boil, beating all the time so that the mixture doesn't stick, then reduce the heat and simmer for about 5 minutes, until golden brown and thick. Pour over the shortbread base and let cool.

To make the chocolate topping, put the chocolate in a heatproof bowl set over a saucepan of barely simmering water and stir gently until melted. Pour the chocolate over the caramel and leave to set. Use a hot knife to cut into 16 squares to serve.

These shortbreads will keep for up to 5 days if stored in an airtight container.

This cookie smells truly delicious as you remove it from the oven – do use culinary lavender, which has not been sprayed with pesticides.

# lavender shortbreads

**115 g/1 stick butter, softened**
**60 g/⅓ cup caster/superfine or granulated sugar, plus extra for dusting**
**85 g/⅔ cup gluten-free plain/all-purpose baking flour**
**2 teaspoons culinary lavender, finely ground**
**85 g/¾ cup ground almonds**
**a little milk, if required**
**almond meal flour, for rolling out**

*2 baking sheets, greased and lined*

Makes 20 shortbreads

Preheat the oven to 180°C (350°F) Gas 4.

Put the butter and sugar in a mixing bowl and cream together until light and creamy. Sift in the flour and add the lavender and ground almonds. Bring together to a dough with your hands. If the mixture is too dry add a little milk to moisten it.

Transfer the dough to a work surface. Roll the dough into a long sausage shape, 5-cm/2-in diameter. Roll in almond meal flour so that it coats the edge of the dough. Chill in the fridge for 30 minutes. Cut into 1-cm/½-in thick slices and arrange on the prepared baking sheets a small distance apart. Press the back of a fork down into each shortbread to make ridges.

Bake in the preheated oven for 12–15 minutes, until golden brown. Remove from the oven and dust with sugar. Let cool on the baking sheets before serving.

These shortbreads will keep for up to 5 days if stored in an airtight container.

These hearty bars, packed with nuts, seeds and dried fruit, are perfect for a quick energy fix. They are ideal for lunchboxes or as after-school treats and contain plenty of natural goodness. You can omit some of the nuts, seeds or fruit, doubling up the quantities of others if you want to customize the recipe. Lexia raisins are extra-large Muscatel raisins and well worth looking out for.

# coconut & pumpkin power bars

**100 g/7 tablespoons butter**
**50 g/¼ extra virgin coconut oil**
**150 g/¾ cup caster/granulated sugar**
**3 tablespoons golden/light corn syrup**
**80 g gluten-free self-raising flour OR ¾ cup gluten-free all-purpose baking flour plus 1 teaspoon baking powder and ⅛ teaspoon xanthan gum**
**2 eggs, beaten**
**150 g/2 cups desiccated coconut**
**100 g/1 cup shelled unsalted pistachios**
**60 g/½ cup pumpkin seeds**
**60 g/½ cup sunflower seeds**
**60 g/½ cup pine nuts**
**150 g/1 cup raisins or sultanas/golden raisins**

*a 30 x 20-cm/12 x 8-in deep-sided baking tin/pan, greased and base-lined*

Makes 14 bars

Preheat the oven to 180°C (350°F) Gas 4.

Put the butter, coconut oil, sugar and syrup in a large saucepan and heat until the butter has melted. Take off the heat and leave to cool slightly.

Sift the flour into a mixing bowl and add all the remaining ingredients. Stir with a wooden spoon until everything is well mixed together. Pour in the cooled butter mixture and mix together.

Tip the mixture into the prepared tin/pan and press down using the back of a spoon. Bake in the preheated oven for 20–25 minutes, until the top is golden brown and the mixture feels firm to the touch. Let cool completely in the tin/pan then tip out onto a chopping board and cut into bars to serve.

These bars will keep for up to 5 days if stored in an airtight container.

The cherry bakewell has been popular in England for many years. Buttery pastry is spread thickly with cherry jam and topped with a baked almond custard. Whilst traditionally made with ground almonds, this recipe is made with coconut, which gives a lovely texture and flavour. Look out for Baker's Edge coconut.

# coconut bakewell slices

***For the base***
**125 g/1 stick plus 1 tablespoon butter, softened**
**100 g/½ cup caster/ granulated sugar**
**1 generous tablespoon golden/light corn syrup**
**150 g/2 cups long soft shredded coconut**
**50 g/⅓ cup coconut flour**
**250 g/1 cup cherry preserve**

***For the topping***
**100 g/7 tablespoons butter**
**100 g/½ cup caster/ granulated sugar**
**3 eggs**
**50 g/⅓ cup gluten-free plain/all-purpose baking flour**
**50 g/⅓ cup coconut flour**
**100 g/1 cup ground almonds**
**150 g/2 cups desiccated coconut**
**2 tablespoons sour cream**

*a 30 x 20-cm/12 x 8-in baking tin/pan, greased and base-lined*

Make 10 slices

Preheat the oven to 180°C (350°F) Gas 4.

To make the base, put the butter, sugar and syrup in a large saucepan and set over low heat until melted. Add the shredded coconut and coconut flour and mix well. Transfer the mixture to the prepared tin/pan and use the back of a spoon to press it down to cover the base of the tin/pan. Use a round-bladed knife to spread over the cherry preserve.

To make the coconut topping, put the butter and sugar in a mixing bowl and whisk until light and creamy. Beat in the eggs, then add both the flours, ground almonds, 100 g/generous 1 cup of the shredded coconut and sour cream and mix well.

Spoon the coconut topping over the preserve layer and spread out evenly. Sprinkle the remaining shredded coconut over the top. Bake in the preheated oven for 30–40 minutes, until golden brown and the topping is set. Remove from the oven and let cool in the tin/pan before cutting into slices to serve.

These slices are best eaten on the day they are made.

These moreish bites have a tangy cheese punch and a delightful smokiness that comes from the chestnut flour. Sprinkled with onion seeds, poppy seeds and salt and pepper, they are good served as a nibble with drinks or used as a canapé base. They couldn't be simpler to make, using an all-in-one method in a food processor.

# cheese bites

**115 g/1 scant cup gluten-free plain/all-purpose baking flour, plus extra for dusting**
**50 g/½ cup chestnut flour**
**75 g/5 tablespoons butter**
**70 g/½ cup grated Cheddar**
**60 g/scant ½ cup grated Emmental**
**1 egg yolk**
**2–3 tablespoons buttermilk**
**1 teaspoon French mustard**
**½ teaspoon Spanish hot smoked paprika**

***To finish***
**1 egg yolk, beaten**
**black onion seeds, poppy seeds, sea salt flakes and cracked black pepper, for sprinkling**

*2 baking sheets, greased and lined*

*a 5-cm/2-in round cutter*

Makes 36 bites

Preheat the oven to 190°C (375°F) Gas 5.

Put both the flours and butter in a food processor and blitz until the butter is finely mixed with the flour and the mixture resembles fine breadcrumbs. Add the Cheddar, Emmental, egg yolk, 2 tablespoons buttermilk, mustard and paprika and blitz again.

Tip the mixture onto a floured work surface and bring together with your hands, adding a little more buttermilk if the mixture is too dry. Dust with a little more flour and use a rolling pin to roll out the dough to a thickness of ½ cm/¼ in. Use the cutter to stamp out 36 rounds and transfer them to the prepared baking sheets. Brush the top of each bite with the beaten egg yolk and sprinkle seeds over the top. You can use a combination of seeds on each one (as shown) or divide the bites into three batches and top each batch with black onion seeds, poppy seeds or with a mix of sea salt flakes and cracked black pepper.

Bake in the preheated oven for 10–15 minutes, until the bites are golden brown. Let cool slightly on the baking sheet then transfer to a wire rack to cool completely.

These bites are best eaten on the day they are made.

# cakes

My German friend Maren introduced me to the delights of buckwheat cake, delicate layers of almost marshmallow-like sponge filled with whipped cream and sour/tart cherries. Based on a recipe from northern Germany, this indulgent cake is similar in style to the ever-popular Black Forest Gâteau.

# buckwheat & cherry cake

**6 large eggs, separated**
**200 g/1 cup caster/ superfine sugar**
**100 g/¾ cup buckwheat flour**
**2 teaspoons baking powder**
**kirsch, for drizzling (optional)**
**600 ml/2½ cups double/heavy cream, whipped to soft peaks**
**300 g/1 cup bottled or canned sour/tart morello cherries (drained weight)**
**3 tablespoons grated dark chocolate**

*a 23-cm/9-in springform cake tin/pan, greased and lined*

Serves 8–10

Preheat the oven to 180°C (350°F) Gas 4.

Whisk together the egg yolks and sugar until thick, pale and creamy. In a separate grease-free bowl, whisk the egg whites to stiff peaks. Gently fold the egg whites into the egg yolk mixture. Mix together the flour and baking powder, sift over the egg mixture and gently fold in.

Pour the batter into the prepared baking tin/pan. Bake in the preheated oven for 30–40 minutes, until the cake is firm to the touch. It will feel foam-like rather than cake-like – almost like a giant marshmallow.

Carefully turn the cake out from the tin/pan onto a wire rack and let cool completely. Using a large, sharp knife, slice the cake into three layers. Drizzle each layer with kirsch, if using. Assemble the cake, filling each layer with whipped cream and cherries. Top the final layer with grated chocolate and serve immediately or cover and refrigerate until needed.

This cake is best eaten on the day it is made as it contains fresh cream. Refrigerate until ready to serve.

This moist carrot and coconut cake is so delicious that you wouldn't know it was gluten-free. The caramel, coconut and ginger topping is rich and buttery, making the cake perfect for dessert, served with a large spoonful of cream. The cake can be served warm or cold (although we tend to eat it as soon as it is removed from the oven as it always smells too delicious to resist).

# carrot & coconut cake

**170 g/1 ½ sticks butter, plus 1 extra tablespoon for the topping**
**170 g/¾ cup plus 1 tablespoon caster/ granulated sugar**
**3 eggs**
**170 g gluten-free self-raising flour OR 1 ⅓ cups gluten-free all-purpose baking flour plus 1 ¼ teaspoons baking powder and ¾ teaspoon xanthan gum**
**200 g/2 scant cups long shredded coconut**
**2 carrots, grated**
**1 apple, cored and grated**
**85 g/½ cup sultanas/golden raisins**
**1 teaspoon ground cinnamon**
**1 teaspoon mixed spice/apple pie spice**
**200 ml/¾ cup buttermilk**
**1 tablespoon ginger syrup**
**2 tablespoons golden/light corn syrup**

*a 20-cm/8-inch round springform cake tin/pan, greased and lined*

Serves 8–10

Preheat the oven to 180°C (350°F) Gas 4.

Cream together the butter and sugar until light and creamy using an electric mixer or whisk. Add the eggs one at a time, beating after each addition. Fold in the flour, half of the shredded coconut, grated carrots and apple, sultanas/golden raisins, cinnamon, mixed spice/apple pie spice and buttermilk, ensuring that everything is incorporated.

Spoon the batter into the prepared tin/pan. Bake in the preheated oven for 40–55 minutes, until the cake is golden brown and springs back to the touch and a knife inserted in the middle comes out clean with no batter on it. If the cake starts to brown too quickly, cover loosely with a sheet of foil.

Meanwhile, to make the topping, put the tablespoonful of butter and both the syrups in a medium saucepan and heat gently until the butter has completely melted. Stir in the remaining shredded coconut and simmer for 2–3 minutes, until the coconut has absorbed some of the syrup.

Remove the cake from the oven, let it cool in the tin for 10 minutes and then turn out onto a wire rack to cool. Spoon the coconut topping evenly over the warm cake and let cool.

This cake will keep for up to 3 days if stored in an airtight container.

Gingerbread was my grandad's favourite cake and my mum would always bake a batch to take with us when we went to visit. I remember it being dark, sticky and laden with treacle/molasses and syrup – just how gingerbread should be.

# apple & orange gingerbread

**115 g/1 stick butter**
**170 g/½ cup black treacle/molasses**
**60 g/scant ¼ cup golden/light corn syrup**
**30 g/2 tablespoons dark soft brown sugar**
**125 ml/½ cup milk**
**2 eggs**
**115 g/¾ cup plus 1 tablespoon gluten-free plain/all-purpose baking flour**
**115 g/1 cup ground almonds**
**1 teaspoon mixed spice/apple pie spice**
**1 teaspoon ground cinnamon**
**2 teaspoons ground ginger**
**1 teaspoon bicarbonate of soda/baking soda**
**1 teaspoon vanilla extract**
**finely grated zest of 2 small oranges**
**1 large apple, cored and grated**
**50 g/⅓ cup flaked/sliced almonds**
**icing/confectioners' sugar, for dusting**

*a 35 x 25-cm/14 x 10-in cake tin/pan, greased and base-lined*

Makes 16 squares

Preheat the oven to 180°C (350°F) Gas 4.

Put the butter, treacle/molasses, syrup and sugar in a saucepan and heat gently until the butter has melted and the sugar dissolved. Whisk in the milk, set aside to cool for 10 minutes then beat in the eggs.

Sift the flour into a mixing bowl and stir in the ground almonds, spices, bicarbonate of soda/baking soda, vanilla extract, orange zest, apple and almonds.

Pour the treacle mixture into the dry ingredients and mix well. Pour the batter into the prepared tin/pan and bake in the preheated oven for 30–40 minutes, until the gingerbread is firm to touch but still soft. Remove from the oven and let cool in the tin/pan. Dust with icing/confectioners' sugar and cut into squares to serve.

This gingerbread will keep for up to 3 days if stored in an airtight container.

I made this cake to take to our village harvest supper – a delightful event where we all enjoy a simple casserole followed by apple cakes and pies for dessert, and an auction of homegrown produce for charity. The cake is topped with my friend Susan's caramel icing – so delicious that I just begged for the recipe until she gave in!

# apple & pecan cake

**200 g/2 cups shelled pecans**
**225 g/2 sticks butter, softened**
**115 g/½ cup caster/ granulated sugar**
**115 g/½ cup dark soft brown sugar**
**4 eggs**
**150 g gluten-free self-raising flour plus 1 teaspoon baking powder OR 1 cup and 2 tablespoons gluten-free all-purpose baking flour plus 2 teaspoons baking powder and ¼ teaspoon xanthan gum**
**2 teaspoons ground cinnamon**
**2 apples**
**100 ml/⅓ cup sour cream**

***For the icing***
**60 g/½ stick butter**
**150 g/¾ cup caster/ superfine sugar**
**2 tablespoons milk**
**2 teaspoons vanilla extract**
**220 g/1½ cups icing/ confectioners' sugar**
**ground cinnamon, for dusting**

*a 25-cm/10-in springform tin/pan, greased and lined*

Serves 10

Preheat the oven to 170°C (325°F) Gas 3.

Blitz the pecans in a food processor until they resemble ground almonds. Whisk together the butter and both sugars until light and creamy. Add the eggs and whisk again. Fold in the flour, baking powder, cinnamon and ground pecans using a spatula or spoon.

Peel, grate and core the apples and fold through the batter, along with the sour cream. Spoon the batter into the prepared cake tin/pan and bake in the preheated oven for 1–1¼ hours, until the cake is firm to the touch and a knife inserted into the middle of the cake comes out clean. Let cool in the tin/pan for a few minutes then turn out onto a wire rack and let cool.

To make the icing, put the butter and sugar in a saucepan and heat gently until the butter has melted and the sugar starts to caramelize. Add the milk and vanilla extract and heat for 1 minute further. Remove from the heat, let cool for 5 minutes, then beat in the icing/confectioners' sugar using a whisk. Spread the icing over the cooled cake using a spatula and sift over a little ground cinnamon.

This cake will keep for up to 5 days if stored in an airtight container.

Here is a deliciously rich chocolate cake made with ground hazelnuts, which give the cake its nutty crunch. Lovers of Nutella hazelnut and chocolate spread will definitely enjoy a slice of this! Serve with freshly whipped cream for an extra-special treat!

# chocolate hazelnut ring

**100 g/7 tablespoons butter, softened**
**140 g/scant 3/4 cup caster/granulated sugar**
**3 eggs**
**150 g/1 1/2 cups blanched hazelnuts**
**100 g/1 cup ground almonds**
**60 g gluten-free self-raising flour plus 1 teaspoon baking powder OR 1/2 cup gluten-free all-purpose baking flour plus 1 1/2 teaspoons baking powder and 1/8 teaspoon xanthan gum**
**140 g/5 oz dark chocolate, melted**
**1 teaspoon vanilla extract**
**3 tablespoons sour cream**

***To decorate***
**100 g/3 1/2 oz dark chocolate, melted**
**50 g/1/2 cup blanched hazelnuts, toasted**

*a 23-cm/9-in springform ring tin/pan, greased*

Serves 10

Preheat the oven to 180°C (350°F) Gas 4.

Cream together the butter and sugar. Whisk in the eggs one at a time. Blitz the hazelnuts to a fine powder in a food processor or chop very finely with a sharp knife.

Add the ground hazelnuts, ground almonds, flour, baking powder, melted chocolate, vanilla extract and sour cream to the bowl and fold through with a spatula until everything is incorporated. Spoon into the prepared tin/pan and bake in the preheated oven for 30–40 minutes, until a knife inserted in the cake comes out clean.

Let the cake cool in the tin for 10 minutes then remove the sides and centre of the tin and let the cake cool on a wire rack. Drizzle the cake with the melted chocolate and sprinkle over the hazelnuts to decorate.

This cake is best eaten on the day it is made.

The classic victoria sponge remains the most popular of English teatime treats. Light vanilla sponge cakes are traditionally sandwiched together with buttercream and strawberry preserve. This delightful recipe replaces the buttercream with whipped cream and fresh, juicy strawberries for an indulgent treat.

# victoria sponge cake

**185 g/1 stick plus 5 tablespoons butter, softened**
**185 g/1 cup less 1 tablespoon caster/ granulated sugar**
**4 eggs**
**200 g/2 cups ground almonds**
**125 g gluten-free self-raising flour OR 1 scant cup gluten-free all-purpose baking flour plus 1 teaspoon baking powder and ¼ teaspoon xanthan gum**
**150 ml/⅔ cup sour cream**
**2 teaspoons vanilla extract**

***To assemble***
**3 generous tablespoons strawberry preserve**
**250 ml/1 cup double/heavy cream, whipped**
**150 g/2 cups hulled and sliced strawberries**
**icing/confectioners' sugar, for dusting**

*two 20-cm/8-in cake tins/pans, greased and base-lined*

Serves 10

Preheat the oven to 180°C (350°F) Gas 4.

Put the butter and sugar in a mixing bowl and whisk until light and creamy. Add the eggs one at a time, whisking after each addition. Add the ground almonds, flour, sour cream and vanilla extract and fold through gently. Spoon the mixture into the prepared cake tins/pans and level using a spatula.

Bake in the preheated oven for 25–30 minutes, until the cakes are firm to the touch and a knife inserted into the middle of each cake comes out clean. Turn out onto a wire rack and let cool completely.

Spread the preserve over one of the cakes. Cover with the whipped cream and strawberry slices and top with the other sponge. Dust with icing/confectioners' sugar and serve immediately or refrigerate until needed.

This cake is best eaten on the day it is made as it contains fresh cream. Refrigerate until ready to serve.

The flavours of almond and chocolate complement each other perfectly in this delicious cake. Sandwiched together with a rich buttercream, this cake would be the ideal centrepiece for afternoon tea or to serve with morning coffee.

# almond & chocolate chip layer cake

**225 g/2 sticks butter, softened**
**225 g/1 cup plus 2 tablespoons caster/ granulated sugar**
**4 eggs, lightly beaten**
**150 g gluten-free self-raising flour plus 2 teaspoons baking powder OR 1 cup and 2 tablespoons gluten-free all-purpose baking flour plus 3 teaspoons baking powder and ¼ teaspoon xanthan gum**
**115 g/1 generous cup ground almonds**
**2 teaspoons almond extract**
**100 g/⅔ cup chocolate chips**
**100 ml/⅓ cup buttermilk**

***For the buttercream***
**60 g/2½ oz. dark chocolate**
**115 g/1 stick butter, softened**
**220 g/1½ cups icing/ confectioners' sugar, plus extra for dusting**
**1 tablespoon buttermilk**

*two 20-cm/8-in round cake tins/pans, greased and lined*

*a piping bag, fitted with a large round nozzle (optional)*

Serves 8–10

Preheat the oven to 180°C (350°F) Gas 4.

Put the butter and sugar in a mixing bowl and whisk together until light and creamy. Add the eggs and whisk again. Sift in the flour and baking powder and add the ground almonds. Use a spatula to fold in. Add the almond extract, chocolate chips and buttermilk and mix until everything is incorporated.

Divide the cake batter between the prepared cake tins/pans. Bake in the preheated oven for 25–35 minutes, until the cakes are golden brown, firm to the touch and a knife inserted in the middle of each cake comes out clean. Transfer to a wire rack to cool.

To make the filling, break the chocolate into pieces and put in a heatproof bowl set over a saucepan of barely simmering water. Take care that the base of the bowl does not touch the water. Stir until the chocolate has melted. Take the bowl off the heat and let the chocolate cool. Whisk in the butter, icing/confectioners' sugar and buttermilk until smooth. Spoon the buttercream into the piping bag and pipe stars on one cake. (If you do not have a piping bag, spread the filling over the cake with a round-bladed knife.) Top with the second cake and lighty dust with icing/confectioners' sugar to serve.

This cake will keep for up to 2 days if stored in an airtight container.

Ripe juicy plums, bursting blueberries and warming cinnamon – this good-looking cake is delicious served with whipped cream on the side.

# plum & cinnamon cake

**185 g/1½ sticks plus 1 tablespoon butter, softened**
**275 g/1½ cups caster/granulated sugar**
**6 eggs**
**125 g gluten-free self-raising flour OR 1 scant cup gluten-free all-purpose baking flour plus 1 teaspoon baking powder and ¼ teaspoon xanthan gum**
**2 teaspoons ground cinnamon**
**400 g/4½ cups ground almonds**
**whipped cream, to serve**

***For the topping***
**8 ripe plums, halved and pitted**
**100 g/1 cup blueberries**
**2 tablespoons caster/granulated sugar**
**icing/confectioners' sugar, for dusting**

*a 25-cm/10-in springform tin/pan, greased and lined*

Serves 10

Preheat the oven to 160°C (325°F) Gas 3.

Put the butter and sugar in a mixing bowl and whisk until light and creamy. Add the eggs one at a time, whisking after each addition. Sift in the flour and cinnamon, add the ground almonds and whisk again. Spoon the batter into the prepared cake tin/pan and level the surface.

Arrange the plums, cut-side up, over the top of the cake, scatter over the blueberries and sprinkle with the sugar.

Bake in the preheated oven for 1½–2 hours, until the cake is firm to the touch and a knife inserted into the middle of the cake comes out clean.

Remove from the oven and let cool in the tin/pan for 10 minutes, then turn out onto a wire rack to cool completely. Dust with icing/confectioner's sugar and serve with whipped cream.

This cake will keep for up to 3 days if stored in an airtight container.

Tangy lemon slices, drenched in a lemon caramel, nestled on top of a delicate lemon sponge, make this cake a must for all citrus lovers. Delicious served warm with custard sauce or cold with whipped cream.

# caramelized lemon cake

**170 g/1½ sticks butter, softened**
**170 g/¾ cup plus 2 tablespoons caster/ granulated sugar**
**3 large eggs**
**115 g gluten-free self-raising flour plus 1 teaspoon baking powder OR heaped ¾ cup gluten-free all-purpose baking flour plus 2 teaspoons baking powder and ¼ teaspoon xanthan gum**
**85 g/¾ cup ground almonds**
**3 tablespoons sour cream**
**custard sauce or whipped cream, to serve**

***For the caramelized lemons***
**200 g/1 cup caster/ granulated sugar**
**freshly squeezed juice of 1 lemon**
**4 lemons**

*a 25-cm/10-in cast iron tarte tatin pan or a similar heavy, flameproof tin/pan, greased*

Serves 8–10

Preheat the oven to 180°C (350°F) Gas 4.

To make the caramelized lemons, put the sugar and lemon juice in a saucepan and heat until the sugar melts and turns golden brown. Do not stir whilst cooking but gently shake the pan from time to time to prevent the sugar from burning. Watch closely once the sugar has melted as it will caramelize quickly. Pour into the bottom of the pan. Grate the zest from 3 of the lemons and reserve for the cake batter. Cut the top and bottom from all 5 lemons and stand them upright on a chopping board. Using a sharp knife slice away the peel and pith in vertical slices and repeat until the lemons are peeled. Cut each lemon into 6 slices and remove any pips using a sharp knife. Arrange the lemon slices in the caramel in the pan in a circular pattern – taking care as the caramel will be hot. Set aside.

Put the butter and sugar in a mixing bowl and whisk together until light and creamy. Beat in the eggs and whisk again until the batter is light and airy. Sift in the flour and baking powder and add the ground almonds, sour cream and reserved lemon zest. Fold together until everything is incorporated. Spoon the batter into the pan with the lemon slices. Bake in the preheated oven for 30–40 minutes, until the cake springs back to the touch and a knife inserted in the middle of the cake comes out clean. Remove from the oven and let cool for a few minutes then put a serving plate on top of the pan and, holding the pan with a kitchen towel (so you do not burn yourself) invert the cake onto the plate. Serve warm or cold with custard sauce or whipped cream.

This cake will keep for up to 2 days if stored in an airtight container.

Banana bread is always popular, especially when served warm from the oven, cut in thick slices and generously spread with butter. The addition of brazil nuts here gives this loaf cake a lovely texture but you can substitute any nuts you prefer – pistachios or hazelnuts both work well.

# banana & brazil nut loaf cake

**2 ripe bananas**
**115 g/1 stick butter, softened**
**115 g/½ cup plus 1 tablespoon caster/granulated sugar**
**2 large eggs**
**115 g gluten-free self-raising flour OR 1 scant cup gluten-free all-purpose baking flour plus 1 teaspoon baking powder and ¼ teaspoon xanthan gum**
**3 tablespoons buttermilk**
**2 teaspoons ground cinnamon**
**1 teaspoon ground mixed spice/apple pie spice**
**100 g/1 cup brazil nuts, coarsely chopped**

***For the caramel glaze***
**1 tablespoon butter**
**1 tablespoon light soft brown sugar**
**1 tablespoon golden/light corn syrup**
**¼ teaspoon fine sea salt**

*two 450-g/1-lb loaf tins/pans, greased and lined*

Makes 2 loaf cakes

Preheat the oven to 180°C (350°F) Gas 4.

Put the bananas in a bowl and mash with a fork. Put the butter and sugar in a mixing bowl and whisk until light and creamy. Add the eggs one at a time, whisking after each addition. Add the mashed banana, flour, buttermilk, cinnamon, mixed spice/apple pie spice and brazil nuts and fold in until everything is incorporated.

Divide the batter between the prepared loaf tins/pans and bake in the preheated oven for 25–30 minutes, until the cakes are firm to the touch and a knife inserted in the middle of each cake comes out clean. Remove the loaves from the oven and let cool slightly while you make the glaze.

To make the salted caramel glaze, heat the butter, sugar, syrup and salt in a saucepan until the butter has melted and the sugar dissolved. Drizzle the caramel over the warm cakes to glaze and leave for a few minutes before turning out onto a wire rack to cool.

These cakes will keep for up to 3 days if stored in an airtight container. They also freeze very well, so if you don't need both cakes, you can freeze one for up to 2 months.

# small bakes

The classic scone is so simple to make but is always popular. Filled with cream, fruit preserve and fresh strawberries, these scones represent everything that is lovely about the British summertime.

# buttermilk scones

**350 g gluten-free self-raising flour plus 2 teaspoons baking powder OR 2½ cups plus 1 tablespoon gluten-free all-purpose baking flour plus 4 teaspoons baking powder and 1 teaspoon xanthan gum**
**100 g/1¼ cups ground almonds**
**115 g/1 stick butter**
**60 g/⅓ cup caster/granulated sugar, plus extra for sprinkling**
**2 teaspoons almond extract**
**200–250 ml/¾–1 cup buttermilk**
**milk, for glazing**

***To serve***
**300 g/1 cup clotted cream**
**3 generous tablespoons strawberry preserve**
**icing/confectioners' sugar, to dust**

*a baking sheet, greased and lined*

*a 7.5-cm/3-in fluted cutter*

Makes 12

Preheat the oven to 190°C (375°F) Gas 5.

Put the flour, baking powder and ground almonds in a mixing bowl and rub in the butter with your fingertips. Add the sugar and almond extract and mix in the buttermilk, until you have a soft dough (you may not need all of it so add it gradually).

Put the dough on a floured work surface and use a rolling pin to roll it out to a thickness of 2–3 cm/¾–1¼ in. Stamp out 12 scones using the cutter. Arrange the scones on the prepared baking sheet so that they are a distance apart. Brush the tops with milk and sprinkle with a little caster/granulated sugar. Bake in the preheated oven for 15–20 minutes, until golden brown and the scones sound hollow when you tap them. Transfer to a wire rack to cool.

To serve, cut the scones in half, spoon some cream on the base of each one, top with preserve and strawberry slices and cover with the tops of the scones. Dust with icing/confectioners' sugar to serve.

These scones are best eaten on the day they are made but can be frozen and reheated before serving.

***Variation*** Try adding 85 g/½ cup dried cherries, sultanas/golden raisins or chocolate chips to the scone dough (replacing the almond extract with vanilla extract).

When autumn/fall comes, I take a basket and head to the hedgerows. There is nothing nicer than picking free produce such as blackberries, hips and crab apples. This delicious recipe uses ripe blackberries with seasonal pears for a rustic scone that's perfect served warm with plenty of creamy butter.

# pear & blackberry scone round

**225 g gluten-free self-raising flour plus 1 teaspoon baking powder OR 1¾ cups gluten-free all-purpose baking flour plus 2 teaspoons baking powder and ½ teaspoon xanthan gum**
**200 g/2 cups ground almonds**
**2 teaspoons ground cinnamon**
**½ teaspoon fine sea salt**
**115 g/1 stick butter, chilled and cubed**
**55 g/¼ cup caster/granulated sugar, plus extra for sprinkling**
**200 ml/¾ cup buttermilk**
**200 g/1 cup blackberries**
**2 ripe pears, peeled, cored and sliced**
**1 egg, beaten**

*a baking sheet, greased and lined*

Makes 8 slices

Preheat the oven to 190°C (375°C) Gas 5.

Put the flour, baking powder, ground almonds, cinnamon and salt in a large mixing bowl and stir together.

Add the butter and rub into the flour with your fingertips, until the mixture resembles fine breadcrumbs. Add the sugar and buttermilk and mix to form a soft dough, adding a little milk if the mixture is too dry. Add the blackberries and pear slices and gently bring the dough together with your hands.

Put the dough on a floured work surface and shape it into a 23-cm/9-in diameter round. Transfer to the prepared baking sheet using a large spatula. Brush the scone round with the beaten egg and sprinkle with a little extra sugar. Using a sharp knife, score the top of the scone into 8 sections but do not cut all the way through the dough. Bake in the preheated oven for 20–25 minutes, until golden brown and the scone sounds hollow when you tap it. Serve warm with butter for spreading.

This scone round is best eaten on the day it is made.

If you are more of a savoury than sweet person, then these are the scones for you. Packed with cheese and walnuts and with the satisfying crunch of poppy seeds, they are delicious served as an accompaniment to a hearty bowl of soup.

# cheese & poppy seed scones

**350 g gluten-free self-raising flour plus 2 teaspoons baking powder OR 2½ cups plus 1 tablespoon gluten-free all-purpose baking flour plus 4 teaspoons baking powder and 1 teaspoon xanthan gum, plus extra flour for dusting**
**100 g/1 cup ground almonds**
**115 g/1 stick butter, chilled and cubed**
**200 g/1½ cups grated Cheddar**
**100 g/1 cup walnut halves, finely chopped**
**2 tablespoons poppy seeds, plus extra for sprinkling**
**1 generous teaspoon French mustard**
**200–250 ml/¾–1 cup buttermilk**
**1 egg yolk, beaten**

*a baking sheet, greased and lined*

*a 7.5-cm/3-in round fluted cutter*

Makes 12 scones

Preheat the oven to 190°C (375°F) Gas 5.

Put the flour, baking powder and ground almonds in a mixing bowl and rub in the butter with your fingertips. Add the grated cheese, walnuts, poppy seeds and mustard and stir in. Mix in the buttermilk, until you have a soft dough (you may not need all of it so add it gradually).

Put the dough on a floured work surface and use a rolling pin to roll it out to a thickness of 2–3 cm/¾-1¼ in. Stamp out 12 rounds using the cutter. Arrange the scones on the prepared baking sheet a small distance apart, brush the tops with the beaten egg and sprinkle with poppy seeds. Bake in the preheated oven for 15–20 minutes, until the scones are golden and sound hollow when you tap them. Serve warm or cold.

These scones are best eaten on the day they are made but can be frozen and reheated before serving.

I was first introduced to pumpkin scones at the wonderful Alice's Tea Rooms in New York and have been hooked ever since. The pumpkin purée, flavoured with maple syrup, cinnamon and vanilla, is what makes these scones really moist.

# pumpkin scones

**300 g/10 oz peeled pumpkin or butternut squash, chopped into 3-cm/1¼-in pieces**
**40 ml/3 tablespoons pure maple syrup**
**2 tablespoons vanilla extract**
**1 teaspoon ground cinnamon**
**350 g gluten-free self-raising flour plus 1 teaspoon baking powder OR 2½ cups plus 1 tablespoon gluten-free all-purpose baking flour plus 3 teaspoons baking powder and 1 teaspoon xanthan gum**
**100 g/1 cup ground almonds**
**115 g/1 stick butter**
**50 g/¼ cup caster/ granulated sugar**

***For the maple glaze***
**40 ml/3 tablespoons maple syrup**
**20 g/1 tablespoon butter**
**40 g/scant ¼ cup caster/ granulated sugar**
**1 teaspoon vanilla extract**

*a baking sheet, greased and lined*

*a 7.5-cm/3-in fluted cutter*

Makes 14

Preheat the oven to 190°C (375°F) Gas 5.

Put the pumpkin pieces on a large piece of double layer of kitchen foil. Drizzle over the maple syrup and vanilla extract and sprinkle with the cinnamon. Wrap the foil up well and transfer to a baking sheet. Bake in the preheated oven for 30–40 minutes, until the pumpkin is soft. Let cool, then purée in a food processor.

Put the flour, baking powder and ground almonds in a mixing bowl and rub in the butter with your fingertips. Add half the pumpkin purée and sugar to the flour and mix in. Gradually add the remaining purée a little at a time, until you have a soft dough. You may not need all the purée, depending on the water content of your pumpkin.

Put the dough on a floured work surface and use a rolling pin to roll out the scone dough to a thickness of 2–3 cm/¾-1¼. Stamp out 14 rounds using the cutter. Arrange the scones on the prepared baking sheet a small distance apart. Bake in the preheated oven for 12–15 minutes, until the scones are golden brown and sound hollow when you tap them.

To make the glaze, put the maple syrup, butter, sugar and vanilla extract in a small saucepan and gently heat until the butter has melted and the sugar dissolves. Brush the glaze over the warm scones using a pastry brush. Serve warm or cold.

These scones are best eaten on the day they are made but can be frozen and reheated before serving.

These little muffins are bursting with fresh blueberries and zingy lemon and have a hidden layer of cream cheese to make them nice and moist. Perfect for brunch or afternoon tea.

# blueberry & lemon muffins

**115 g/1 stick butter, softened**
**115 g/½ cup plus 2 tablespoons caster/granulated sugar**
**2 eggs, beaten**
**85 g gluten-free self-raising flour plus 1 teaspoon baking powder OR ¾ cup gluten-free all-purpose baking flour plus 2 teaspoons baking powder and ¼ teaspoon xanthan gum**
**1 teaspoon bicarbonate of soda/baking soda**
**60 g/¾ cup ground almonds**
**80 ml/⅓ cup buttermilk**
**grated zest of 2 lemons**
**100 g/1 cup blueberries**
**3 tablespoons cream cheese**
**freshly squeezed juice of 2 lemons**
**3 tablespoons icing/confectioners' sugar**

*a 12-hole muffin tin/pan, lined with paper cases*

Makes 12

Preheat the oven to 180°C (350°F) Gas 4.

Put the butter and sugar in a mixing bowl and whisk together until light and creamy. Add the eggs and whisk again. Fold in the flour, baking powder, bicarbonate of soda/baking soda, ground almonds, buttermilk, lemon zest and blueberries. Put a spoonful of batter in each paper case to half fill it and then put 1 teaspoon of cream cheese in each one. Top with another spoonful of the cake batter, ensuring that the cream cheese is completely covered.

Bake in the preheated oven for about 15–20 minutes, until the muffins are firm to the touch.

To make the lemon drizzle, heat the lemon juice in a small saucepan with the icing/confectioners' sugar and pour over the muffins whilst they are still warm. Let the muffins cool in the tin/pan before serving.

These muffins are best eaten on the day they are made.

Cornmeal flour gives these delicious muffins a lovely golden colour. Bursting with fresh apricots, chocolate and cherries and brushed with an apricot butter glaze, they are great for lunchboxes and picnics.

# apricot cornmeal muffins

**100 g/¾ cup cornmeal flour**
**150 g gluten-free self-raising flour plus 1 teaspoon baking powder OR 1⅓ cups gluten-free all-purpose baking flour plus 2¼ teaspoons baking powder and ¾ teaspoon xanthan gum**
**100 g/½ cup caster/granulated sugar**
**100 g/1 cup ground almonds**
**200 ml/¾ cup milk**
**1 teaspoon vanilla extract**
**2 generous tablespoons plain Greek yogurt**
**100 g/7 tablespoons butter, melted and cooled**
**2 large eggs**
**2 tablespoons apricot preserve**
**7 fresh apricots**
**75 g/½ cup dried sour cherries**
**100 g/3½ oz dark chocolate, finely chopped**

***For the apricot glaze***
**2 tablespoons apricot preserve**
**1 tablespoon butter**

*a 12-hole muffin tin/pan, lined with paper cases*

Makes 12

Preheat the oven to 180°C (350°F) Gas 4.

Put the cornmeal flour, flour, baking powder, sugar and ground almonds in a mixing bowl.

Put the milk, vanilla extract, yogurt and melted butter in a separate bowl and whisk together. Add the eggs and apricot preserve to the milk mixture and whisk again. Pour the milk mixture into the bowl containing the dry ingredients and fold in with a large spoon.

Pit the apricots and chop 5 of them into small pieces. Stir the chopped apricots, cherries and chocolate into the batter. Divide the batter between the paper cases. Cut the remaining apricots into thin slices and arrange 2 on top of each muffin. Bake in the preheated oven for 15–20 minutes, until risen and golden brown.

To make the glaze, heat the apricot preserve and butter in a small saucepan and then brush over the warm muffins with a pastry brush. Leave to cool slightly then transfer to a wire rack to cool completely.

These muffins are best eaten on the day they are made.

These savoury muffins, packed with walnuts, cheese and sweetcorn, make a delicious breakfast snack and are a great accompaniment to soups. You can replace the walnuts with other nuts if you prefer and add different ingredients, such as cooked, diced bacon pieces or sun-dried tomatoes.

# cheese & sweetcorn muffins

**150 g gluten-free self-raising flour plus 1 teaspoon baking powder OR 1⅓ cups gluten-free all-purpose baking flour plus 2¼ teaspoons baking powder and ¾ teaspoon xanthan gum**
**1 teaspoon bicarbonate of soda/baking soda**
**200 g/2 cups shelled walnuts, ground**
**165 g/⅔ cup canned sweetcorn**
**200 g/2 cups grated Cheddar**
**150 ml/⅔ cup milk**
**4 rounded tablespoons crème fraîche or sour cream**
**100 g/7 tablespoons butter, melted**
**2 eggs**
**1 generous teaspoon wholegrain mustard**
**2 teaspoons sugar**
**sea salt and freshly ground black pepper**

*a 12-hole muffin tin/pan, lined with paper cases*

Makes 10–12 muffins

Preheat the oven to 180°C (350°F) Gas 4.

Sift the flour, baking powder and bicarbonate of soda/baking soda into a mixing bowl, add the ground walnuts and mix well. Drain the sweetcorn and stir in to the mixture, along with 150 g/1½ cups of the cheese.

Put the milk, crème fraîche, melted butter, eggs, mustard and sugar in a separate bowl. Season with salt and pepper and whisk together. Pour the milk mixture into the bowl containing the dry ingredients and fold in with a large spoon. The batter should be thick and slightly lumpy. Divide the batter between the paper cases. Bake in the preheated oven for 15–20 minutes, until golden brown and firm to the touch. Five minutes before the end of cooking, remove the muffins from the oven, sprinkle over the remaining cheese and return to the oven. Serve warm or cold.

These muffins are best eaten on the day they are made.

Lemon and almond are a match made in heaven. The drizzle ensures that these little loaf cakes stay nice and moist and the icing and almond topping finish them off to perfection.

# lemon & amaretto loaf cakes

**115 g/1 stick butter, softened**
**115g/½ cup plus 1 tablespoon caster/ granulated sugar**
**2 large eggs**
**60 g gluten-free self-raising flour OR ½ cup gluten-free all-purpose baking flour plus ½ teaspoon baking powder and ⅛ teaspoon xanthan gum**
**60 g/½ cup ground almonds**
**80 ml/⅓ cup plain yogurt**
**grated zest of 2 lemons**

***For the drizzle***
**60 ml/¼ cup amaretto**
**1 tablespoon caster/ superfine sugar**
**freshly squeezed juice of 2 lemons**

***For the icing***
**160 g/1 cup icing/ confectioners' sugar**
**freshly squeezed juice of 2 lemons**
**flaked/sliced almonds**

*6 mini loaf tins/pans, greased and lined*

Makes 6 mini loaf cakes

Preheat the oven to 180°C (350°F) Gas 4.

Put the butter and sugar in a mixing bowl and whisk until light and creamy. Add the eggs and whisk again. Fold in the flour, ground almonds, yogurt and lemon zest using a spatula. Put a large spoonful of cake batter into each prepared tin/pan. Bake in the preheated oven for about 20–25 minutes, until the cakes are firm to the touch and golden brown.

To make the drizzle, put the amaretto, sugar and lemon juice in a small saucepan and heat until the sugar has dissolved. Pour over the warm cakes and leave to cool in the tins/pans.

To make the icing, mix the icing/confectioner's sugar and lemon juice together, adding a little extra water if the icing is too stiff. Remove the cakes from the tins, spoon a little icing over the top of each cake and sprinkle with almonds.

These cakes will keep for up to 2 days if stored in an airtight container.

There are few more pleasing cakes than the madeleine. Whilst they may look quite humble, flavour- and texture-wise they are a delight and ideal to serve with coffee or as an accompaniment to mousses and other creamy desserts. These are flavoured with honey, orange and cinnamon and eating them always transports me to the souks of Marrakesh. The secret to achieving the perfect texture is to chill the batter before baking – this helps the cakes to rise and be as light as a feather.

# honey madeleines

**2 eggs**
**80 g/⅓ cup plus 2 tablespoons caster/granulated sugar**
**70 g gluten-free self-raising flour plus 1 teaspoon baking powder OR ½ cup plus 1 tablespoon gluten-free all-purpose baking flour plus 1½ teaspoons baking powder and ⅛ teaspoon xanthan gum**
**50 g/½ cup ground blanched hazelnuts**
**1 tablespoon honey**
**grated zest of 1 orange**
**1 teaspoon cinnamon**
**100 g/7 tablespoons butter, melted and cooled**
**icing/confectioners' sugar, for dusting**

*a piping bag, fitted with a large round nozzle/tip*

*2 madeleine tins/pans, very well greased with butter*

Makes about 16

Put the eggs and sugar in a mixing bowl and whisk until light and creamy. Sift in the flour and baking powder and add the hazelnuts, honey, orange zest and cinnamon. Whisk again. Pour in the cooled melted butter and fold in using a spatula until everything is incorporated. Spoon into a piping bag.

Chill the mixture in the fridge for 1 hour, taking care that the piping bag is well secured so that the mixture doesn't leak. The best way to do this is to wrap the open end of the nozzle in clingfilm/plastic wrap and then sit the piping bag upright in a large jug/pitcher.

Preheat the oven to 180°C (350°F) Gas 4. Pipe some of the mixture into each of the madeleine moulds/molds so that they are filled level. Bake in the preheated oven for 10–15 minutes, until golden brown. (If you have only one madeleine pan, bake in batches, storing the uncooked batter in the fridge whilst the first batch is cooking.) Gently remove the madeleines from the pan and transfer to a wire rack to cool. Dust with a little icing/confectioners' sugar whilst still warm.

These cakes are best eaten on the day they are made.

This interpretation of the dainty little fondant fancy cake is inspired by one of my favourite childhood sweets/candies – coconut ice – layers of pink and white coconut. Coconut lovers, these cakes are for you!

# coconut ice fancies

**115 g/1 stick butter, softened**
**115 g/½ cup plus 1 tablespoon caster/ granulated sugar**
**2 large eggs**
**85 g gluten-free self-raising flour OR ¾ cup gluten-free all-purpose baking flour plus 1 teaspoon baking powder and ⅛ teaspoon xanthan gum**
**30 g/scant ⅓ cup coconut flour**
**60 g/¾ cup desiccated coconut**
**125 ml/½ cup buttermilk**

***For the buttercream***
**1 tablespoon solid virgin coconut oil**
**30 g/2 tablespoons butter, softened**
**70 g/½ cup icing/ confectioners' sugar, sifted**
**½ tablespoon buttermilk**
**2 tablespoons coconut rum, to drizzle (optional)**

***To decorate***
**3 tablespoons desiccated coconut**
**pink food colouring**
**100 g/¾ cup icing/confectioners' sugar**

*a 20-cm/8-in square baking tin/pan, greased and lined*

Makes 8 fancies

Preheat the oven to 180°C (350°F) Gas 4.

To make the sponge cake, put the butter and sugar in a mixing bowl and whisk until light and creamy. Add the eggs and whisk again. Fold in the flour, coconut flour, desiccated coconut and buttermilk using a spatula or large spoon. Spoon the batter into the prepared tin/pan and bake in the preheated oven for 20–30 minutes, until the cake is golden brown and springs back to your touch. Turn out onto a wire rack and let cool.

To make the buttercream, bring the solid coconut oil to room temperature and put in a bowl. Add the butter, icing/ confectioners' sugar and buttermilk and beat for several minutes until you have a smooth, whipped frosting.

Using a sharp knife, slice away the edges of the cake to neaten then cut it in half down the middle. Put half the cake on a tray that will fit in the fridge. Drizzle the coconut rum over the top (if using) and spread with a thin layer of buttercream. Put the other half on top and cover the top with more buttercream, smoothing with a round-bladed knife. Put the cake in the fridge for 1 hour to allow the buttercream to set.

To decorate, put the coconut in a bowl and stir in a few drops of pink food colouring. Mix the icing/confectioners' sugar with 1–2 tablespoons water – a little at a time as you may not need it all. Cut the cake into 8 squares and put them on a wire rack with a sheet of foil underneath to catch any drips. Spoon the icing over each one. Let the icing set for a few minutes then sprinkle each cake with pink coconut. Let icing set completely before serving.

These fancies will keep for up to 2 days if stored in an airtight container.

Everyone loves a cupcake. These are bursting with cranberries and white chocolate and topped with a pretty swirled buttermilk frosting – perfect for any celebration.

# cranberry & white chocolate cupcakes

**60 g/½ stick butter, softened**
**60 g/⅓ cup caster/granulated sugar**
**1 egg**
**60 g gluten-free self-raising flour plus 1 teaspoon baking powder OR ½ cup gluten-free all-purpose baking flour plus 1½ teaspoons baking powder and ⅛ teaspoon xanthan gum**
**30 g/⅓ cup pecans, finely ground**
**60 g/½ cup dried cranberries**
**50 g/⅓ cup white chocolate buttons/chips**
**2 tablespoons buttermilk**

***For the frosting***
**220 g/1½ cups icing/confectioners' sugar**
**115 g/1 stick butter, softened**
**1 teaspoon vanilla extract**
**1 tablespoon buttermilk**
**pink food colouring**
**sprinkles of your choice**

*a 12-hole cupcake tin/pan, lined with paper cases*

*a piping bag, fitted with a large star nozzle/tip*

Makes 12

Preheat the oven to 180°C (350°F) Gas 4.

Put the butter and sugar in a mixing bowl and whisk until light and creamy. Add the egg and whisk again. Fold in the flour, baking powder, ground pecans, cranberries, chocolate buttons and buttermilk using a spatula or large spoon. Divide the batter between the paper cases. Bake in the preheated oven for 15–20 minutes, until the cakes are golden brown and spring back to the touch. Transfer to a wire rack to cool.

To make the frosting, sift the icing/confectioners' sugar into a mixing bowl and add the butter, vanilla extract and buttermilk. Beat together until you have a thick frosting. Put half the frosting in a separate bowl and mix in a few drops of pink food colouring. Spoon the frosting into the piping bag, spreading the pink one along one side of the bag and the cream one along the other side so that when you squeeze it the frosting is striped. Pipe a generous swirl of frosting onto each cooled cake, add some sprinkles and dust with icing/confectioners' sugar.

These cupcakes are best eaten on the day they are made.

Red velvet cake – the signature dish of the Waldorf Astoria in New York in the 1920s – is coloured red to give it its distinctive look. Not quite a vanilla cake, not quite a chocolate cake, but most definitely delicious and a firm favourite with many people. Topped with a swirl of cream cheese frosting, these cupcakes are just impossible to resist!

# red velvet cupcakes

**115 g/1 stick butter**
**115 g/½ cup plus 1 tablespoon caster/ granulated sugar**
**2 eggs**
**85 g gluten-free self-raising flour plus 1 teaspoon baking powder OR ¾ cup gluten-free all-purpose baking flour plus 2 teaspoons baking powder and ⅛ teaspoon xanthan gum**
**60 g/½ cup ground almonds**
**50 g/2 oz. dark chocolate, melted**
**150 ml/⅔ cup buttermilk**
**red food colouring**

***For the frosting***
**240 g/1¾ cups icing/ confectioners' sugar**
**60 g/½ stick butter, softened**
**70 g/⅓ cup cream cheese**
**1 tablespoon buttermilk**
**gluten-free cocoa powder, for dusting**

*a 12-hole cupcake tin/pan, lined with paper cases*

*a piping bag fitted with a large star nozzle/tip*

Makes 12 cupcakes

Preheat the oven to 180°C (350°F) Gas 4.

Put the butter and sugar in a mixing bowl and whisk until light and creamy. Add the eggs and whisk again. Fold in the flour, baking powder, ground almonds, melted chocolate and buttermilk using a spatula or large spoon. Beat in some red food colouring, a drop at a time, until the batter is a dark, reddish brown. Divide the cake batter between the paper cases. Bake in the preheated oven for 15–20 minutes, until the cakes are firm to the touch and a knife inserted into the middle of a cake comes out clean.
Transfer to a wire rack to cool.

To make the frosting, sift the icing/confectioners' sugar into a mixing bowl and add the butter, cream cheese and buttermilk. Beat together until you have a thick frosting. Spoon the frosting into the piping bag and pipe a large swirl on top of each cooled cake. Dust with a little sifted cocoa powder to decorate.

These cupcakes are best eaten on the day they are made.

# breads & yeast doughs

Making gluten-free bread dough is very different to making regular bread dough. The steps to creating this tasty loaf couldn't be simpler as it requires no kneading and no proving. This bread keeps well if stored in an airtight container and is delicious for ham and mustard sandwiches. You can also substitute other flavours in place of the cheese and onion seeds if you prefer.

# crusty cheese & onion bread

**250 g gluten-free self-raising flour plus 3 teaspoons baking powder OR 2 scant cups gluten-free all-purpose flour plus 4 teaspoons baking powder and ½ teaspoon xanthan gum**
**3 eggs, beaten**
**50 g/3½ tablespoons butter, melted and cooled**
**280 ml/1 cup plus 2 tablespoons buttermilk**
**60 g/generous ½ cup grated Gruyère**
**60 g/generous ½ cup grated Cheddar**
**1 tablespoon black onion seeds**
**1 tablespoon snipped chives**
**3 tablespoons finely grated Parmesan**

*a 9-in springform cake tin/pan, greased and lined*

Makes 1 round loaf

Preheat the oven to 180°C (350°F) Gas 4.

Sift the flour and baking powder into a mixing bowl. Add the eggs, melted butter and buttermilk. Fold in the Gruyère and Cheddar, together with the onion seeds and chives, until everything is mixed together well.

Spoon the mixture into the prepared tin/pan – the mixture will be quite sticky and resemble cake batter rather than traditional bread dough.

Sprinkle the Parmesan over the top and bake in the preheated oven for 40–50 minutes, until the top of the loaf is golden and springs back to your touch. Let cool in the tin/pan for about 5 minutes before turning out onto a wire rack to cool completely.

This bread will keep for up to 3 days if stored in an airtight container.

The delicious Italian focaccia bread is perfect in summer, topped with fresh seasonal ingredients, perhaps from your garden – juicy tomatoes, perfumed sprigs of fresh rosemary and olives.

# rosemary, olive & tomato focaccia

**2 teaspoons fresh yeast**
**2 teaspoons honey**
**2 tablespoons warm water**
**450 g gluten-free white bread flour OR 3½ cups gluten-free all-purpose baking flour plus 1½ teaspoons xanthan gum**
**300 ml/1 cup plus 3 tablespoons warm milk**
**2 eggs, beaten**
**1 teaspoon vinegar**
**3 tablespoons buttermilk**
**1 teaspoon fine sea salt**
**20 cherry tomatoes, halved**
**20 pitted black olives, halved**
**sprigs of fresh rosemary**
**olive oil, for drizzling**
**sea salt flakes**

*a 33 x 23-cm/13 x 9-inch shallow-sided baking tin/pan, greased with olive oil*

Makes 1 large loaf

Put the yeast, honey and warm water in a cup and leave for 10–15 minutes, until the mixture becomes foamy.

Sift the flour into a mixing bowl and add the yeast mixture, warm milk, eggs, vinegar, buttermilk and fine salt and whisk together until everything is incorporated. Spoon the mixture into the prepared tin/pan, cover with a clean, damp kitchen towel and leave in a warm place for 1 hour, until the dough has doubled in size and risen.

When the dough has risen, preheat the oven to 190°C (375°F) Gas 5. Press the tomatoes, olives and rosemary into the top of the mixture, drizzle with olive oil and sprinkle with sea salt flakes. Bake in the preheated oven for about 30–40 minutes, until the bread springs back to the touch and has a crusty top.

This bread is best eaten warm on the day it is made.

This golden yellow bread, studded with sweetcorn kernels, yellow (bell) pepper, chilli and coriander/cilantro is perfect comfort food. Simply scrumptious served still warm direct from the oven and great with soup or a bowl of chilli con carne.

# sunshine cornbread

Preheat the oven to 190˚C (375˚F) Gas 5.

Mix together the polenta flour, flour and bicarbonate of soda/baking soda, then stir in the sweetcorn, yellow (bell) pepper, paprika and ground chillies.

Whisk together the buttermilk, butter and eggs and season with salt and pepper. Add to the dry ingredients and mix everything together. Fold in the chopped coriander/cilantro. Pour the mixture into the prepared tin/pan and level the surface with a spatula.

Bake in the preheated oven for 30–40 minutes, until the loaf is golden brown on top.

This bread is best eaten warm on the day it is made.

**300 g/2 cups fine ground polenta/cornmeal or corn/maize flour (masa harina)**
**60 g gluten-free self-raising flour OR 6 tablespoons gluten-free all-purpose baking flour plus ½ teaspoon baking powder**
**2 teaspoons bicarbonate of soda/baking soda**
**165 g/¾ cup canned sweetcorn kernels (drained weight)**
**1 yellow (bell) pepper, deseeded and finely chopped**
**¼ teaspoon hot paprika**
**2 dried bird's-eye/bird chillies, ground**
**570 ml/2¼ cups buttermilk**
**1 heaped tablespoon very soft butter**
**2 eggs**
**3 tablespoons chopped fresh coriander/cilantro**
**sea salt and freshly ground black pepper**

*a 30 x 20-cm/12 x 8-inch roasting tin/pan, greased and lined*

Makes 1 large loaf

These little rolls are kept moist by the addition of puréed baked potato. They are an ideal accompaniment to soup and are delicious served as breakfast rolls. If you are short of time, you can boil the potatoes but I prefer the flavour that baked potatoes give the rolls. If you do boil them, make sure that they are well drained before you mash them otherwise the dough mixture will be too wet.

# potato rolls

- **4 small potatoes (about 300 g/10½ oz. combined weight), baked and cooled**
- **150 g/1 stick plus 2 tablespoons butter, softened**
- **20 g/1½ tablespoons caster/granulated sugar**
- **2 eggs, beaten**
- **170 g gluten-free self-raising flour plus 1 teaspoon baking powder OR 1⅓ cups gluten-free all-purpose baking flour plus 2¼ teaspoons baking powder and ¾ teaspoon xanthan gum**
- **½ teaspoon fine sea salt**

*a 12-hole muffin tin/pan, greased with butter*

*an ice cream scoop*

Makes 10 rolls

Preheat the oven to 180°C (350°F) Gas 4.

Scoop the baked potatoes from their skins, put in a food processor and blitz to a smooth purée. If you do not have a food processor, use a potato masher and mash to remove all the lumps. Set aside to cool.

Whisk together the butter and sugar then beat in the eggs. Sift in the flour and baking powder, add the salt and cooled potato purée and whisk until everything is well incorporated.

Put an ice cream scoop of the potato mixture in 10 of the holes in the muffin tin/pan. Bake in the preheated oven for 20–25 minutes, until golden and crisp.

These rolls are best eaten warm on the day they are made.

My Gujarati sisters-in-law; Tanu and Manda, helped me develop this recipe based on a classic Indian gram flour bread. These flatbreads are ideal to serve cut into slices with dips in place of a pitta bread, or two of them can be filled with grated cheese and grilled for the perfect cheese melt. You can also add a variety of spices or herbs to the dough – finely chopped rosemary and thyme or Indian spices if you are serving as an accompaniment to curries and dhals.

# flatbreads

**200 g/1⅔ cups gluten-free plain/all-purpose baking flour**
**100 g/1⅓ cups gram (chickpea) flour**
**1 teaspoon fine sea salt**
**1 tablespoon sunflower or vegetable oil, plus extra for cooking (optional)**
**1 generous tablespoon plain yogurt**

Makes 8 flatbreads

Sift the plain/all-purpose flour into a mixing bowl and add the gram flour and salt. Pour in the oil and yogurt then add 60–80 ml/¼–⅓ cup water gradually, mixing with your hands until you have a ball of dough – you may not need all of the water. The dough should not be sticky at all and should be firmer than normal bread dough.

Divide the dough into 8 balls of equal size (about the size of a golf ball). Put them on a floured work surface and use a rolling pin to roll each ball out to a thin 20-cm/8-in round.

Heat a dry frying pan/skillet until hot. Cook the breads one at a time for 2–3 minutes on one side then turn over and cook for a further 1–2 minutes on the other side, until lightly golden brown. If you wish, add a little oil to the pan towards the end of cooking so that the breads are lightly fried, which adds to the taste. For best cooking results, press down on the breads during cooking with a clean heatproof towel, which squeezes out the air and causes the breads to puff up slightly.

These breads are best eaten on the day they are made.

***Variation*** To make spiced flatbreads add ½ teaspoon ground chilli, 1 teaspoon ground cumin and 1 teaspoon ground coriander, or 1 teaspoon garam masala or medium curry powder to the dough. Check that your spices do not contain any gluten before using.

What gives a classic bagel its chewy texture and shiny coat is boiling it in water prior to baking. Unfortunately, given the fragile nature of gluten-free dough, this method just results in disintegration – bye bye bagel! I found the solution is to just submerge the bagels in boiling water, allowing them to float for a few seconds. The resulting bagels have a good chewy texture and are delicious toasted or filled.

# onion seed bagels

**150–200 ml/⅔–¾ cup warm water**
**1 tablespoon gluten-free fast-action dried yeast**
**1 tablespoon white caster/granulated sugar**
**450 g/3½ cups gluten-free plain/all-purpose baking flour**
**2 whole eggs plus 1 whisked egg white**
**1 tablespoon black onion seeds, plus extra for sprinkling**
**2 tablespoons plain yogurt**

*2 baking sheets, lined with non-stick baking parchment*

Makes 10

Put the warm water, yeast and sugar in a bowl and leave for 5–10 minutes, until the mixture is foamy. Sift the flour into a mixing bowl and add the 2 whole eggs. Pour in the yeast mixture and add the onion seeds and yogurt. Mix with your hands to form a soft, moist dough.

Divide the dough into 10 pieces of equal size and roll them into small balls. Press your thumb into the middle of the ball to make the bagel hole, smoothing the edges with your finger and using extra flour if the dough is too sticky to work. Arrange them a distance apart on the prepared baking sheets, cover with oiled clingfilm/plastic wrap and leave in a warm place for 1 hour.

Preheat the oven to 180°C (350°F) Gas 4. Fill a roasting tin/pan with boiling water and carefully transfer it to the bottom of the oven – this will create steam. Fill a large, deep heatproof dish with boiling water. Put a bagel on a slotted spoon and lower it into the water for about 10 seconds, until the bagel lifts off the spoon and floats. Use the spoon to remove it from the water and return it to the baking sheet. Repeat with the remaining bagels. When all the bagels have been in the water, brush them with a little egg white and sprinkle with onion seeds. Bake in the preheated oven for 20–30 minutes, until golden brown on top and underneath.

These bagels are best eaten on the day they are made.

***Variation*** For cinnamon and raisin bagels, replace the onion seeds with 2 teaspoons cinnamon and 100 g/⅝ cup raisins. When the bagels are brushed with egg white, sprinkle with caster/superfine sugar mixed with more cinnamon.

Stollen is a deliciously rich and buttery fruit bread, which is said to have originated in 14th-century Germany. Traditionally stollen are cooked in special pans, which give the loaves their classic shape, but if you haven't got a stollen pan you can just shape the dough into a loaf on the baking sheet with your hands.

# spiced stollen

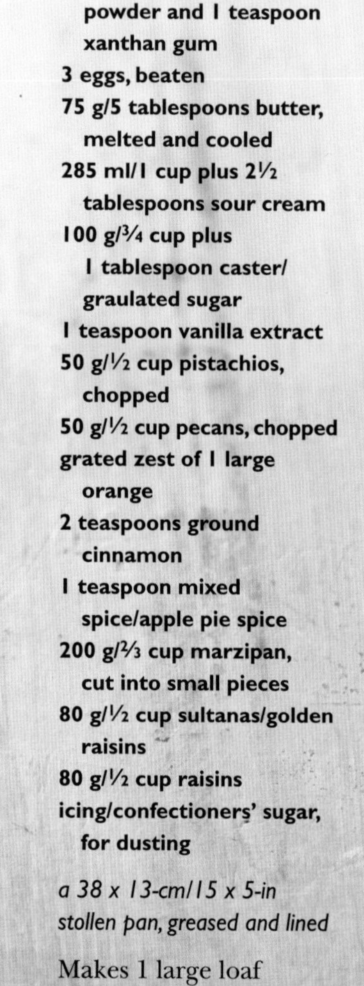

**250 g gluten-free self-raising flour plus 3 teaspoons baking powder OR 2 scant cups gluten-free all-purpose baking flour plus 5 teaspoons baking powder and 1 teaspoon xanthan gum**
**3 eggs, beaten**
**75 g/5 tablespoons butter, melted and cooled**
**285 ml/1 cup plus 2½ tablespoons sour cream**
**100 g/¾ cup plus 1 tablespoon caster/ graulated sugar**
**1 teaspoon vanilla extract**
**50 g/½ cup pistachios, chopped**
**50 g/½ cup pecans, chopped**
**grated zest of 1 large orange**
**2 teaspoons ground cinnamon**
**1 teaspoon mixed spice/apple pie spice**
**200 g/⅔ cup marzipan, cut into small pieces**
**80 g/½ cup sultanas/golden raisins**
**80 g/½ cup raisins**
**icing/confectioners' sugar, for dusting**

*a 38 x 13-cm/15 x 5-in stollen pan, greased and lined*

Makes 1 large loaf

Preheat the oven to 180°C (350°F) Gas 4.

Sift the flour and baking powder into a mixing bowl. Add the eggs with 3½ tablespoons of the melted butter, sour cream and sugar. Stir in the vanilla extract, pistachios, pecans, orange zest, spices, marzipan, sultanas/golden raisins and raisins. Spoon the batter into the prepared pan and then invert onto a baking sheet so that the dough is covered by the pan. If you do not have a stollen pan, shape the dough into a long oval loaf, about 35 x 20 cm/14 x 8 in, dusting your hands with flour as you work.

Bake in the preheated oven for 40–50 minutes, until the top of the stollen is golden, gently lifting away the pan (if using) to see if it is cooked. Brush the cooked loaf with the remaining melted butter and dust with icing/confectioners' sugar, which will be absorbed by the butter to give the loaf a sugary coating.

This stollen will keep for up to 5 days if stored in an airtight container.

These doughnuts are an extra-special treat and the variations are endless too! Pop a square of chocolate in the middle of each doughnut when shaping, or add the grated zest of two lemons to the dough and fill with lemon curd for a tangy treat.

# cinnamon maple doughnuts

**2 teaspoons fast-action dried yeast**
**100 ml/⅓ cup warm water**
**90 g/scant ½ cup caster/ granulated sugar**
**350 g gluten-free self raising flour OR 2½ cups plus 1 tablespoon gluten-free all-purpose baking flour plus 2 teaspoons baking powder and 1 teaspoon xanthan gum**
**a pinch of fine sea salt**
**200 g/2 cups ground almonds**
**60 g/½ stick butter, chilled and cubed**
**1 egg**
**1 tablespoon maple syrup**
**2 teaspoons ground cinnamon**
**1½ tablespoons sour cream**
**about 1 litre/4 cups vegetable oil**
**caster/superfine sugar mixed with ground cinnamon, for dusting**
**about 300 g/1 cup plum preserve (optional)**

*a baking sheet, greased*

*a piping bag, fitted with a jam/jelly nozzle/tip (optional)*

Makes 20 doughnuts

Put the yeast, warm water and 1 tablespoon of the sugar in a small bowl and leave in a warm place for 5–10 minutes, until a foam forms on top.

Sift the flour into a mixing bowl, add the salt and ground almonds and rub in the butter with your fingertips. Add the egg, maple syrup, cinnamon, sour cream and yeast mixture and mix with your hands. Knead gently to form a soft, pliable dough – adding a little flour if the mixture is too sticky.

Divide the mixture into 20 balls of equal size. Put them on the prepared baking sheet, cover with oiled clingfilm/ plastic wrap and leave in a warm place for about 1 hour, until the doughnuts have increased in size.

Heat the oil in a large saucepan – you will need sufficient oil to allow the doughnuts to float slightly above the base to ensure even cooking. To test whether the oil is hot enough, add a scrap of the dough to the pan – if it sizzles, floats to the top and turns golden brown the oil is ready. Cook the doughnuts in small batches for about 3–5 minutes on each side, until they are golden brown.

Mix the caster/superfine sugar and cinnamon together on a plate and position it near to your saucepan. Remove the cooked doughnuts from the pan with a slotted spoon, drain on paper towels and roll in the cinnamon sugar. Leave to cool on a sheet of baking parchment.

If you are filling the doughnuts, pass the preserve through a fine-meshed sieve/strainer to remove any lumps, then spoon into the piping bag. Squeeze a little into each doughnut. This is easiest done whilst the doughnuts are still warm (but not hot), taking care that you don't overfill.

These doughnuts are best eaten on the day they are made.

# pastry

I have yet to meet a person who doesn't enjoy profiteroles. These light choux buns are filled with cream and crushed fresh raspberries and are served drizzled with a rich chocolate sauce – delicious! I've found that choux pastry works extremely well with gluten-free flour and your guests won't be able to tell the difference.

# raspberry & chocolate profiteroles

***For the choux pastry***
**65 g/½ cup gluten-free plain/all-purpose baking flour**
**50 g/3½ tablespoons butter**
**2 large eggs, beaten with 2 teaspoons vanilla extract**

***For the filling***
**250 ml/1 cup double/heavy cream**
**150 g/1 cup raspberries**
**1 generous tablespoon icing/confectioners' sugar, sifted**

***For the chocolate sauce***
**50 g/2 oz dark chocolate**
**50 ml/scant ¼ cup double/heavy cream**
**1 tablespoon golden/light corn syrup**
**1 tablespoon butter**

*a piping bag fitted with a large round nozzle/tip*

*2 baking sheets, greased and lined with baking parchment*

Makes 20 profiteroles

Preheat the oven to 200°C (400°F) Gas 6.

To make the choux buns, sift the flour twice to remove any lumps. Heat the butter in a saucepan with 150 ml/⅔ cup cold water, until the butter is melted. Bring to the boil, then shoot in the flour all in one go (very quickly) and remove from the heat. Beat hard with a wooden spoon until the dough forms a ball and no longer sticks to the sides of the pan. Leave to cool for about 5 minutes. Add the eggs a small amount at a time and use a balloon whisk to beat them into the dough. The mixture will form a sticky paste which holds its shape when you lift the whisk up. Spoon into the piping bag and pipe 20 balls of dough onto the prepared baking sheets. With clean hands, wet your finger and smooth down any peaks so that the pastry is smooth. Bake in the preheated oven for 12 minutes, then use a sharp knife to puncture each bun to allow the steam to escape. Return them to the oven for a further 2–5 minutes, until crisp. Cool on a wire rack and then cut in half.

Whip the cream to stiff peaks, fold in the raspberries and icing/confectioners' sugar and use to fill the profiteroles.

To make the chocolate sauce, put all the ingredients in a saucepan and heat, stirring, until melted. Serve the filled profiteroles immediately, with the warm sauce spooned over the top.

These profiteroles are best eaten on the day they are made as they contain fresh cream.

These delicate light pastries, filled with dessert wine and honey-poached nectarines are a real treat in summer when the fruits are in season. You can substitute peaches or apricots in place of the nectarines if you prefer.

# nectarine & cream choux rings

- **1 quantity Choux Pastry dough (see page 110)**
- **50 g/½ cup flaked/sliced almonds**
- **3 ripe nectarines, pitted and thickly sliced**
- **125 ml/½ cup sweet dessert wine**
- **1 tablespoon honey**
- **1 teaspoon vanilla extract**
- **250 ml/1 cup double/heavy cream**
- **1 generous tablespoon icing/confectioners' sugar, plus extra for dusting**

*2 piping bags, 1 fitted with a large round nozzle and the other fitted with a large star nozzle/tip*

*a baking sheet, greased and lined with baking parchment*

Makes 12 rings

Preheat the oven to 200°C (400°F) Gas 6.

Spoon the choux pastry dough into the piping bag fitted with a round nozzle/tip and pipe 12 rings of choux pastry onto the prepared baking sheet. With clean hands wet your finger and smooth down any peaks from the piping so that the pastry is smooth. Sprinkle with flaked/sliced almonds.

Bake in the preheated oven for 15 minutes, then use a sharp knife to puncture each ring to allow the steam to escape. Return them to the oven for a further 5 minutes, until crisp. Cool on a wire rack and then cut in half.

Put the nectarines in a saucepan with the wine, honey and vanilla extract. Simmer over gentle heat for 5 minutes. Leave to cool completely.

Whip the cream to stiff peaks, sift in the icing/confectioners' sugar and whisk in. Spoon the cream into the piping bag fitted with a star nozzle/tip and pipe a ring of cream onto the base of each choux ring.

Drain the poached nectarines and cut into small pieces with a sharp knife. Arrange a few on top of the cream. Top with the remaining choux halves and dust with icing/confectioners' sugar. Serve immediately or cover and refrigerate until needed.

These choux rings are best eaten on the day they are made as they contain fresh cream.

# toffee pecan tart

**150 g/¾ cup caster/ granulated sugar**
**150 g/⅔ cup dark soft brown sugar**
**2 generous teaspoons ground cinnamon**
**2 teaspoons vanilla extract**
**100 g/7 tablespoons butter**
**5 generous tablespoons golden/light corn syrup**
**60 ml/scant ¼ cup maple syrup**
**3 eggs**
**300 g/3 cups pecans, finely chopped**

***For the pastry***
**250 g/2 cups gluten-free plain/all-purpose baking flour**
**50 g/½ cup ground almonds**
**100 g/7 tablespoons butter, chilled**
**100 g/½ cup cream cheese**
**50 g/¼ cup caster/ granulated sugar**
**1 egg yolk**
**1 teaspoon vanilla extract**

*a 23-cm/9-in loose-based flan tin/pan, greased and lined*

Makes 12 slices

To make the pastry, sift the flour into a mixing bowl and stir in the ground almonds. Rub in the butter until the mixture resembles fine breadcrumbs. Add the cream cheese, sugar, egg yolk and vanilla extract and use your fingers to mix together to a soft dough, adding a little cold water if the mixture is too dry. Wrap in clingfilm/plastic wrap and chill in the fridge for 1 hour.

Preheat the oven to 180°C (350°F) Gas 4. Put both the sugars, cinnamon, vanilla extract, butter, and both syrups in a saucepan and gently heat until the sugar has dissolved and the butter melted. Remove the pan from the heat and let the mixture cool for 10 minutes before beating in the eggs. Strain the syrup mixture into a measuring jug – you should have about 600 ml/2⅓ cups of toffee syrup.

Bring the pastry to room temperature and break it into small pieces. Put the pieces in the prepared tin/pan and press out evenly with your fingertips, until the base is covered with a thin layer of pastry and there are no gaps. Trim away any excess pastry from around the top edge of the tin/pan. Fill the pastry case with the pecans and pour over 500 ml/2 cups of the syrup mixture so that the nuts are covered and the pastry case almost full. Bake in the preheated oven for 20–30 minutes, until the filling is set and the pastry golden brown. Gently reheat the remaining syrup and brush over the top of the tart whilst it is still warm using a pastry brush.

This tart will keep for up to 3 days if stored in an airtight container.

Pecan pie is *the* classic American dessert. This recipe has crunchy pecan nuts enrobed in rich buttery caramel with hints of cinnamon and vanilla, all encased in a cream cheese pastry. Serve warm or cold with cream.

When my friend Lucy was diagnosed with wheat intolerance, her partner David adapted his mum's family apple pie recipe to be gluten-free and very kindly shared his recipe with me for this book. It is always popular and whenever served, every last crumb disappears. It is best served warm with crème fraîche or Greek yogurt.

# David's apple streusel pie

**3 large cooking apples, peeled and cored**
**caster/granulated sugar, too taste**
**175 g/1¾ cups ground almonds**
**175 g/¾ cup dark soft brown sugar**
**1 generous teaspoon ground cinnamon**
**175 g/1 stick plus 4 tablespoons unsalted butter, cubed**

***For the pastry***
**115 g/¾ cup plus 1 tablespoon gluten-free plain/all-purpose baking flour**
**115 g/scant 1 cup almond flour**
**50 g/⅓ cup icing/ confectioners' sugar**
**115 g/1 stick butter, chilled and cubed**
**2 egg yolks**

*a 23-cm/9-in loose-based, deep fluted tart tin/pan, greased*

*baking beans*

Serves 10

To make the pastry, sift the flours and icing/confectioners' sugar into a mixing bowl. Rub the butter in with your fingertips or blitz in a food processor. Add the egg yolks and bring the dough together with your hands, adding a little water if necessary or extra flour if the dough is too soft. Wrap in clingfilm/plastic wrap and chill for at least 1 hour.

Preheat the oven to 180°C (350°F) Gas 4. Coarsely grate the chilled pastry into the prepared tart tin/pan and press it out with your thumbs, until the sides and base of the tin are covered with the pastry and there are no gaps. Prick the base with a fork and put in the freezer for 30 minutes. Line with baking parchment, fill with baking beans and bake in the preheated oven for 10–15 minutes.

Thinly slice the apples and put them in a saucepan with 1–2 tablespoons cold water. Cover with a tight-fitting lid and stew until very soft. Sweeten to taste with sugar, let cool slightly and then spoon into the blind-baked pastry case.

To make the topping, put the ground almonds, brown sugar and cinnamon in a food processor and blitz. Add the butter and blitz again to a paste. Take small balls of the mixture, press them between your finger and thumb to flatten and arrange them in an overlapping tiled pattern on top of the apple layer. Bake in the preheated oven for 40–50 minutes, until the topping is brown but still soft to the touch. Let cool slightly before serving.

This pie will keep for up to 5 days if refrigerated in an airtight container.

These dainty tartlets are the height of sophistication – crisp buttery pastry filled with real vanilla crème pâtissière and topped with glazed strawberries – they are the perfect accompaniment to a glass of chilled champagne at a summer party.

# strawberry tartlets

**1 tablespoon cornflour/cornstarch**
**60 g/scant ⅓ cup caster/granulated sugar**
**1 egg plus 1 egg yolk**
**100 ml/⅓ cup milk**
**150 ml/⅔ cup double/heavy cream**
**1 vanilla pod/bean, split lengthwise**
**300 g/1½ cups strawberries, hulled and halved**
**5 tablespoons apricot preserve**
**freshly squeezed juice of 2 small lemons**

***For the pastry***
**250 g/2 scant cups gluten-free plain/all-purpose baking flour plus 1 teaspoon xanthan gum**
**50 g/½ cup plus 3 tablespoons ground almonds**
**100 g/7 tablespoons butter, chilled**
**100 g/½ cup cream cheese**
**50 g/¼ cup caster/granulated sugar**
**1 egg yolk**
**1 teaspoon vanilla extract**
**grated zest of 1 lemon**

*an 8-cm/3-in cutter*

*two 12-hole tartlet tins/pans, greased*

*baking beans*

*a piping bag, fitted with a large round nozzle/tip*

Makes 24 tartlets

To make the pastry, sift the flour into a mixing bowl and stir in the ground almonds. Rub in the butter until the mixture resembles fine breadcrumbs. Add the cream cheese, sugar, egg yolk, vanilla extract and lemon zest and mix to a soft dough with your fingers, adding a little water if the dough is too dry or extra flour if it is too sticky. Wrap in clingfilm/plastic wrap and chill for 1 hour.

Preheat the oven to 180°C (350°F) Gas 4. Dust a work surface with flour and use a rolling pin to roll out the pastry to a thickness of 3 mm/⅛ in. Stamp out 24 rounds with the cutter and press one into each hole of the prepared tin/pan. Line the pastry cases with baking parchment, fill with baking beans and bake in the preheated oven for 12–15 minutes, until golden brown and crisp. Let cool on a wire rack.

To make the crème pâtissèrie, put the cornflour/cornstarch, sugar, egg and egg yolk in a bowl and whisk until creamy. Put the milk, cream and vanilla pod/bean in a saucepan and bring to the boil. Pour the hot milk over the egg mixture, whisking continuously. Return to the pan and cook for about 2 minutes, until thick. Remove the vanilla pod, pass the mixture through a sieve/strainer and let cool. Spoon the cooled crème pâtissière into the piping bag and fill the pastry cases. Arrange some strawberry halves on top. Put the preserve and lemon juice in a saucepan and heat until runny, pass through a sieve/strainer, let cool slightly, then brush over the top of each tartlet to glaze using a pastry brush.

These tartlets are best eaten on the day they are made.

If there was one recipe in this book that I wrestled with for a long time it was this one! I knew it was going to be difficult, but even I was surprised when my attempts were more 'brick-like' than delicate leaves of millefeuille pastry. After weeks of trying I finally found a recipe that worked – more by chance than by any scientific process. It is not made in the same way as traditional puff pastry so the process may seem a little strange but it is the best method I have found for thin leaves of pastry and I'm delighted to be able to share it with you here!

# blackcurrant & vanilla slices

**300 ml/1¼ cups double/ heavy cream, whipped**
**4 generous tablespoons blackcurrant preserve**
**icing/confectioners' sugar, for dusting**

***Puff pastry***
**200 g/1¾ sticks butter, chilled**
**175 g/1⅓ cups plus 1 tablespoon gluten-free plain/all-purpose baking flour sifted, plus extra for dusting**
**1 teaspoon xanthan gum**
**2 teaspoons freshly squeezed orange juice**
**1 teaspoon almond extract**
**80–100 ml/¼–⅓ cup cold water**

*2 large baking sheets, greased and lined*

*a piping bag fitted, with a large star nozzle/tip*

Makes 8 slices (about 400 g/14 oz puff pastry dough)

Cut half of the butter into small cubes and mix into the flour using a free-standing mixer or whisk. Add 80–100 ml/¼–⅓ cup cold water, together with the xanthan gum, orange juice and almond extract. You may not need all the water so add gradually. Mix until you have a soft (but not sticky) dough.

Coarsely grate the remaining butter and keep it chilled until required. Lay a large piece of baking parchment on a clean work surface and dust liberally with flour. Using a flour-dusted rolling pin, roll out the pastry to a 50 x 18-cm/20 x 7-in rectangle. Sprinkle half of the grated butter over the pastry and dust liberally with flour. Fold one of the short ends of the pastry up into the middle of the pastry at third intervals. Next take the other thin end of the pastry and fold that down over the already folded pastry so that your pastry is folded into about a third of the size that it was originally and you have a 20 x 18-cm/8 x 7-in rectangle. Dust the surface and rolling pin with more flour, turn the pastry over and roll out into a 50 x 18-cm/20 x 7-in rectangle again, with the folds in the same direction as they were originally rolled (and not rotated as you would with traditional puff pastry). Sprinkle the rolled out pastry with the remaining grated butter, dust again with flour and repeat the folding steps. Dust the surface and rolling pin again and repeat the rolling out stages twice more (without adding any butter but still dusting with flour), each time ensuring that the folds and the direction you are rolling out are the same. This helps to ensure that the layers rise. For best results, use the pastry straightaway.

Preheat the oven to 180°C (350°F) Gas 4. Trim any rough edges and then cut out 16 rectangles, each about 8 x 5 cm/3¼ x 2 in and 2.5–5 mm/⅛–¼ in thickness. It is important to use a downward cutting motion with the knife rather than dragging it through the pastry as this may compress the pastry leaves, resulting in less rising of the pastry. Transfer to the baking sheets. Bake in the preheated oven for 10–15 minutes, until the pastry is golden brown and risen. Let cool on a wire rack. Spread 8 of the slices with a few spoonfuls of preserve. Spoon the cream into the piping bag and pipe large stars on top of the cream. Dust with icing/confectioners' sugar and serve immediately or refrigerate until needed. These slices are best eaten on the day they are made as they contain fresh cream.

Here plums and almonds sit atop thin layers of puff pastry and are brushed with a toffee glaze. If you want to use this pastry for savoury dishes omit the orange juice and almond extract and add a teaspoon of mustard to enhance the flavour.

# plum & almond puffs

**1 quantity Puff Pastry (see page 121)**
**plenty of gluten-free plain/all-purpose baking flour, for dusting**
**6–8 ripe red plums, pitted and thinly sliced**
**2 tablespoons caster/superfine sugar**
**2 tablespoons flaked/slivered almonds**

***For the honey glaze***
**50 g/3½ tablespoons butter**
**50 g/¼ cup vanilla sugar**
**1 tablespoon honey**
**1 teaspoon ground cinnamon**

***To serve***
**icing/confectioners' sugar, for dusting**
**whipped cream (optional)**

*2 large baking sheets, greased and lined*

Serves 2–4

Preheat the oven to 180°C (350°F) Gas 4.

Dust a clean work surface with flour and roll out the pastry into a rectangle about 40 x 20 cm/16 x 8 in and to a thickness of about 3–5 mm/⅛ x ¼ in. Trim the edges using a sharp knife. It is important to use a downward cutting motion with the knife rather than dragging it through the pastry as this may compress the pastry leaves, resulting in less rising of the pastry. Cut the rectangle in two and transfer to the baking sheets. (You can make one large slice if you prefer but the pastry is quite fragile and is easier to transfer in two smaller slices.) Using a sharp knife, score a thin line around each pastry slice, about 1 cm/½ in from the edge.

Cover the inner square with thin slices of plum and sprinkle with the caster/superfine sugar and almonds. Make sure that you do not cover the scored line as this will prevent the pastry from rising. Bake in the preheated oven for 20–25 minutes, until the pastry is golden brown and has risen.

Meanwhile make the honey glaze. Put the butter, sugar, honey and cinnamon in a small saucepan with 1 tablespoon water. Heat until the sugar has dissolved and the mixture is smooth and syrupy. When the slices are cooked, remove them from the oven and brush each with the toffee glaze. Serve warm with whipped cream.

These puffs are best eaten on the day they are made.

These tasty cheese pastry tartlets, filled with sweet and sour caramelized onions and a slice of melted Brie, make great canapés. If you prefer, you can make 6 larger tarts in 12-cm/5-in tart tins/pans, which are the perfect size for a starter/appetizer or lunch. Top with fresh thyme or thyme flowers if you have them in the garden.

# brie & caramelized onion tartlets

**3 red onions, thinly sliced (about 350 g/12 oz)**
**30 g/2 tablespoons butter**
**1 tablespoon olive oil**
**2 tablespoons balsamic vinegar**
**40 g/scant ¼ cup caster/granulated sugar**
**1 teaspoon ground allspice**
**150 g/5½ oz brie**
**a few sprigs of fresh thyme**
**sea salt and freshly ground black pepper**

***For the cheese pastry***
**60 g/½ cup gluten-free plain/all-purpose baking flour, sifted, plus extra for dusting**
**30 g/½ cup chestnut flour, sifted**
**40 g/3 tablespoons butter, chilled**
**70 g/½ cup grated Cheddar**
**1 egg yolk**
**1 tablespoon buttermilk**
**1 teaspoon mustard**

*two 12-hole tartlet tins/pans, greased with butter*

*baking beans*

*an 8-cm/3-in round cutter*

Makes 16 tartlets

To make the pastry, put both the flours in a food processor. Add the butter and cheese and blitz until the mixture resembles fine breadcrumbs. Tip into a bowl and add the egg yolk, buttermilk and mustard and mix together to form a soft dough. If the dough is too dry add a little water and if it is too sticky add a little extra flour. Form the dough into a ball, wrap in clingfilm/plastic wrap and chill for 1 hour.

Preheat the oven to 180°C (350°F) Gas 4. Dust a work surface with flour and use a rolling pin to roll out the pastry to a thickness of 3 mm/⅛ in. Stamp out 16 rounds using the cutter and press them into the holes in the prepared tin/pan. Line each pastry case with baking parchment, fill with baking beans and bake in the preheated oven for 10–15 minutes, until the pastry is crisp and golden.

Meanwhile, make the onion filling. Put the onions in a large frying pan/skillet with the butter and oil. Season and cook over gentle heat, until the onions are caramelized and golden brown, adding a little water if the onions start to brown too much. Add the vinegar, sugar and allspice and cook until the sugar has dissolved and the onions are sticky. Let cool, then put a spoonful of onions in each pastry case. Cut the brie into 16 pieces of equal size and put a slice on top of each tartlet. Bake in the oven at 180°C (350°F) Gas 4 for about 5–10 minute, until the cheese starts to melt. Remove the tartlets from the tins/pans and top with sprigs of thyme. Season with black pepper and serve warm or cold.

These tartlets are best eaten on the day they are made.

# desserts

This light almond sponge cake, topped with fresh peaches and crunchy almonds, makes a comforting dessert served with whipped cream or custard sauce. I use Marcona almonds as their rich smoky taste really enhances the sweet peaches.

# peach & almond cake

**170 g/1 stick plus 4 tablespoons butter, softened**
**200 g/1 cup caster/granulated sugar**
**3 large eggs**
**115 g gluten-free self-raising flour OR ¾ cup plus 1 tablespoon gluten-free all-purpose baking powder plus 1 teaspoon baking powder and ½ teaspoon xanthan gum**
**145 g/1½ cups ground almonds**
**150 ml/⅔ cup buttermilk**
**freshly squeezed juice and zest of 1 small orange**
**1 teaspoon vanilla extract**
**4 ripe peaches, pitted and sliced**
**60 g/⅓ cup large whole blanched almonds, such as Marcona**

***For the glaze***
**freshly squeezed juice of 2 lemons**
**3 tablespoons peach preserve**

*a 30 x 20-cm/12 x 8-in rectangular flan tin/pan, greased and lined*

Serves 8–10

Preheat the oven to 180°C (350°F) Gas 4.

Put the butter and 170 g/¾ cup of the sugar in a mixing bowl and cream together. Whisk in the eggs one at a time. Add the flour, ground almonds and buttermilk and fold together with a large spoon. Add the orange juice, zest and vanilla extract and mix until everything is incorporated.

Spoon the cake batter into the prepared tin/pan and arrange the peach slices evenly over the top of the cake. Sprinkle over the almonds and remaining sugar and bake in the preheated oven for 30–40 minutes, until a knife inserted into the middle comes out clean.

Put the lemon juice and peach preserve in a small saucepan and heat gently until the preserve has melted. Strain through a fine mesh sieve/strainer and use a pastry brush to brush it over the top of the cake to glaze. Let the cake cool in the tin/pan then cut into slices to serve.

This cake will keep for up to 2 days if stored in an airtight container.

U.S.

This rich chocolate torte, delicately perfumed with ground pistachios, is a perfect dessert to serve at a dinner party as it can be prepared in advance. To make it extra special why not serve the homemade pistachio ice cream on the side, for the ultimate pistachio treat.

# chocolate torte with pistachio ice cream

***For the torte***

**260 g/9½ oz dark chocolate**
**100 g/7 tablespoons butter**
**200 g/1½ cups icing/confectioners' sugar, plus extra for dusting**
**4 eggs, separated**
**1 teaspoon vanilla extract**
**100 g/1 scant cup shelled pistachios, finely ground**

***For the pistachio ice cream***

**3 egg yolks**
**90 g/5 tablespoons caster/granulated sugar**
**100 ml/⅓ cup milk**
**200 ml/¾ cup double/heavy cream**
**100 g/scant 1 cup shelled pistachios, finely chopped**
**½ teaspoon vanilla extract**
**green food colouring (optional)**

*a 23-cm/9-in springform cake tin/pan, greased and lined*

*an ice cream maker*

Serves 8–10

Preheat the oven to 180°C (350°F) Gas 4.

To make the torte, put the chocolate in a heatproof bowl set over a pan of barely simmering water. Add the butter and melt, stirring occasionally. Remove the bowl from the heat and let cool.

Sift the icing/confectioners' sugar into a mixing bowl and add the egg yolks. Whisk until light, creamy and doubled in size. Fold in the melted chocolate mixture, vanilla extract and ground pistachios. Put the egg whites in a greasefree bowl and whisk until softly peaking. Gently fold the egg whites into the chocolate mixture, making sure everything is incorporated. Pour the batter into the prepared cake tin/pan. Bake in the preheated oven for 25–30 minutes, until a crust has formed on the top of the cake but it is still slightly soft underneath. It will set as it cools so let the cake cool completely in the tin/pan before removing it.

To make the ice cream, whisk together the egg yolks and sugar until thick and creamy. Put the milk, cream and pistachios in a saucepan and bring to the boil. Pour the hot milk and cream over the eggs, whisk together, then return to the pan and cook for a few minutes, until thickened. Add the vanilla extract and a few drops of green food colouring (if using). Let cool, then churn in an ice cream maker until frozen, following the manufacturer's instructions.

Dust the cooled torte with icing/confectioners' sugar and cut into slices. Serve with a scoop of ice cream on the side.

This torte will keep for up to 3 days if stored in an airtight container.

When ripe pears are in season they make delicious desserts. Here they are poached in ginger and vanilla and nestled in a moist almond sponge. Perfection.

# pear & almond sponge

**225 g/2 sticks butter, softened**
**170 g/1 cup caster/ granulated sugar**
**85 g/¾ cup (packed) dark brown sugar**
**100 g/⅓ cup gluten-free marzipan**
**4 eggs**
**115 g gluten-free self-raising flour OR 1 scant cup gluten-free all-purpose baking flour plus 1 teaspoon baking powder and ½ teaspoon xanthan gum**
**200 g/2½ cups ground almonds**
**100 g/½ cup stem ginger in syrup, finely chopped**
**6 tablespoons buttermilk**
**icing/confectioners' sugar, for dusting**

***For the pears***
**5 tall ripe pears, peeled**
**80 ml/⅓ cup ginger syrup**
**100 ml/⅓ cup ginger wine**
**100 g/½ cup caster/ granulated sugar**
**½ vanilla pod/bean, split**
**2 pieces of stem ginger**

*a 23-cm/9-in springform cake tin/pan, greased and lined*

Serves 10

Put the pears in a saucepan with the ginger syrup, ginger wine, sugar, vanilla pod/bean and seeds, stem ginger and enough water so that the pears just float. Simmer for about 20–30 minutes, until the pears are soft. (The actual time needed will depend on how ripe the pears are.) Leave them to cool in the poaching liquid until completely cold. Scoop out the cores from the base of each pear using a melon baller. Discard the cores, return the pears to the poaching liquid and set aside.

Preheat the oven to 180°C (350°F) Gas 4. Put the butter and both sugars in a mixing bowl and whisk together. Cut the marzipan into small pieces and mix into the butter mixture. Add the eggs one at a time, whisking after each addition, until the batter is light and airy. Sift in the flour and add the almonds, stem ginger and buttermilk. Whisk until everything is incorporated. Spoon the batter into the prepared tin/pan.

Drain the pears and arrange them upright in a ring in the tin/pan, pushing each pear all the way down into the cake batter.

Bake in the preheated oven for 35–45 minutes, checking halfway through cooking to ensure that the pears are still upright, adjusting them with a knife if they have slipped. If the cake starts to brown too much, cover loosely with kitchen foil.

Let cool in the tin/pan. Dust with icing/ confectioners' sugar and cut the cake so that each slice contains half a pear.

This cake will keep for up to 3 days if stored in an airtight container.

Delicate friand cakes, made extra light with whisked egg whites, are perfect served with warm griddled pineapple, flambéed in coconut rum and topped with a refreshing scoop of coconut ice cream.

# friands with flambéed pineapple & coconut ice cream

**60 g/⅔ cup desiccated coconut**
**115 g/1 stick butter, softened**
**115 g/½ cup plus 1 tablespoon caster/granulated sugar**
**2 large eggs, separated**
**60 g/½ cup ground almonds**
**2 tablespoons coconut rum**
**2 rings of canned pineapple, finely chopped**
**1 teaspoon vanilla extract**

***For the coconut ice cream***
**3 egg yolks**
**150 g/¾ cup caster/granulated sugar**
**400 ml/1⅓ cups coconut milk**
**250 ml/1 cup double/heavy cream**
**60 ml/¼ cup coconut rum**

***For the flambéed pineapple***
**1 small pineapple, peeled and cut into wedges**
**1 tablespoon dark soft brown sugar**
**100 ml/⅓ cup coconut rum**

*a 12-hole cupcake tin/pan, greased with butter*

*an ice cream maker*

Makes 12 friands

Preheat the oven to 180°C (350°F) Gas 4.

To make the friands, put the coconut in a food processor and blitz until very finely ground. Put the butter, sugar and egg yolks in a mixing bowl and beat together until light and creamy. Whisk in the coconut and ground almonds, coconut rum, pineapple and vanilla extract. Put the egg whites in a separate greasefree bowl and whisk until stiffly peaking. Fold them into the cake batter, adding a third of the egg whites to loosen the mixture and then folding in the remainder. Divide the batter between the holes in the prepared tin/pan and bake in the preheated oven for 20–25 minutes, until the friands are golden brown. Let cool in the tin/pan.

To make the ice cream, put the egg yolks and sugar in a mixing bowl and whisk until thick and creamy. Put the coconut milk and cream in a saucepan and bring to the boil. Pour over the egg mixture, whisking continuously. Add the coconut rum and return the mixture to the pan and cook for 2–3 minutes, until the mixture starts to thicken. Let cool, then churn in an ice cream maker until frozen, following the manufacturer's instructions.

Heat a griddle pan until very hot. Cook the pineapple wedges for 2–3 minutes on each side, sprinkling with the brown sugar when you turn them. Pour over the rum – if you are cooking on a gas flame, take care as the rum will flambé. Serve the friands with some griddled pineapple and a scoop of coconut ice cream on the side. Serve immediately.

The friands will keep for up to 2 days if stored in an airtight container.

I love cheesecake of all types but best of all is a plain baked vanilla cheesecake. This version, based loosely on the classic New York cheesecake, is delicious served with fresh berries. The recipe contains oats, which are not suitable for all those with a gluten intolerance, but gluten-free oats are available so do use these. Alternatively, omit the base altogether and replace the oats with toasted coconut or make a simple crumb base using gluten-free cookies and melted butter.

# baked vanilla cheesecake

***For the base***

**100 g/7 tablespoons butter**

**5 tablespoons golden/light corn syrup**

**250 g/1½ cups gluten-free porridge/rolled oats**

**60 g/⅓ cup caster/granulated sugar**

***For the cheesecake***

**4 eggs**

**600 g/2½ cups cream cheese**

**400 ml/1⅓ cups sour cream**

**140 g/scant ¾ cup caster/granulated sugar**

**225 g/1 cup clotted or extra thick double/heavy cream**

**1 vanilla pod/bean, split**

**2 tablespoons icing/confectioners' sugar**

*a 20-cm/8-in springform tin/pan, greased and lined*

Serves 10

Preheat the oven to 160°C (325°F) Gas 3.

To make the base, put the butter and syrup in a large saucepan and melt over low heat. Stir in the oats and sugar, mixing well to ensure that all the oats are coated. Transfer the mixture to the prepared tin/pan and use the back of a spoon to press it down.

Put the eggs, cream cheese, 100 ml/⅓ cup of the sour cream, sugar, clotted/heavy cream and seeds from the vanilla pod/bean in a mixing bowl and whisk to combine.

Pour the mixture into the tin/pan on top of the base. Bake in the preheated oven for 1–1¼ hours, until the cheesecake is set but still wobbles slightly. Put the remaining sour cream and icing/confectioners' sugar in a bowl and whisk together. Remove the cheesecake from the oven and pour the sour cream mixture over the top. Return it to the oven and bake for a further 10 minutes. Let the cheesecake cool completely in the tin/pan then chill in the fridge before cutting into slices to serve.

This cheesecake will keep for up to 3 days if refrigerated in an airtight container.

I have fond childhood memories of toffee apples – biting through the crisp candy coating to find the juicy apple inside. This cheesecake captures all of those flavours.

# toffee apple cheesecake

**4 small dessert apples, peeled and cored**
**100 g/scant ½ cup dark brown sugar**
**freshly squeezed juice of ½ a lemon**
**85 g/½ cup sultanas/golden raisins**
**2 tablespoons double/heavy cream**
**400 ml/1⅓ cups sour cream**
**250 g/1 cup cream cheese**
**500 g/2 cups mascarpone**
**50 g/¼ cup caster/ granulated sugar**
**4 large eggs, beaten**
**1 teaspoon vanilla extract**
**3 tablespoons gluten-free self-raising flour OR 3 tablespoons gluten-free all-purpose baking flour plus ¼ teaspoon baking powder**

***For the topping***
**4 apples, peeled, cored and sliced**
**freshly squeezed juice of 1 lemon**
**115 g/½ cup dark soft brown sugar**
**60 g/½ stick butter**
**1 tablespoon golden/light corn syrup**
**150 ml/⅔ cup double/heavy cream**

*a 23-cm/9-in springform tin/pan, greased and lined*

Serves 8–10

To make the cheesecake, chop the dessert apples into 1-cm/½-in pieces and put them in a large saucepan. Add the brown sugar, lemon juice, sultanas/golden raisins and 2 tablespoons cold water. Heat until the liquid is syrupy and the apple soft. Stir in the double/heavy cream and simmer for a further 2–3 minutes. Set aside to cool completely.

Preheat the oven to 180°C (350°F) Gas 4. Put the sour cream, cream cheese, mascarpone, caster/granulated sugar, eggs, vanilla extract and flour in a mixing bowl and beat until smooth and creamy. Fold in the cooled apple mixture.

Wrap the edges and base of the baking tin/pan with clingfilm/plastic wrap to make it watertight. Put it in a roasting tin/pan half-filled with boiling water. Pour the cheesecake mixture into the baking tin/pan and bake in the water bath in the preheated oven for 30–40 minutes, until the top of the cheesecake is golden brown and wobbles very slightly when shaken. Remove from the water bath and leave in the pan to cool completely.

To prepare the apple topping, put the apple slices in a saucepan with the lemon juice and 100 ml/⅓ cup of water and simmer until soft. Drain any excess water and let cool. Put the sugar, butter and syrup in a small saucepan and heat gently, until the sugar has dissolved. Add the cream and simmer for a few minutes further, until you have a thick toffee sauce. Serve slices of the cheesecake topped with the apple slices and a generous drizzle of the toffee sauce.

This cheesecake will keep for up to 3 days if refrigerated in an airtight container.

Crumble is the ultimate in comfort food desserts – here tangy plums with a hint of almond and vanilla, are buried beneath a buttery, melt-in-the-mouth crumble.

# plum & amaretto crumble

**800 g/1¾ lb ripe red plums, halved and pitted**
**1 vanilla pod/bean**
**85 g/⅓ cup plus 2 tablespoons caster/granulated sugar**
**100 ml/⅓ cup amaretto or other almond-flavoured liquor**

***For the crumble topping***
**115 g/1 cup ground almonds**
**115 g/1 stick butter, chilled and cubed**
**115 g/⅔ cup gluten-free porridge/rolled oats**
**60 g/⅓ cup caster/granulated sugar**

*a large baking dish, buttered*

Serves 8

Preheat the oven to 180°C (350°F) Gas 4.

Put the plums in a large saucepan. Split the vanilla pod/bean in half lengthwise with a sharp knife and use the tip of the knife to scrape the seeds directly into the saucepan. Add the vanilla pod/bean, sugar and amaretto. Simmer the plums over gentle heat for about 5 minutes, until softened. Remove and discard the vanilla pod/bean and transfer the fruit to the prepared baking dish.

To make the crumble topping, put the ground almonds in a mixing bowl and rub in the butter. Stir in the oats and sugar. Sprinkle the mixture over the plums and bake in the preheated oven for 35–40 minutes, until the topping is golden brown and the plum juices are bubbling around the edge of the dish. Serve warm or cold with cream.

This crumble is best eaten on the day it is made but can be refrigerated for up to 2 days.

Warm caramel, cinnamon and baked bananas – this is one of the most comforting desserts there is. Served with fresh whipped cream, enhanced with tropical coconut rum, this cake is a big hug on a plate!

# banana cake with rum cream

**215 g/1 cup plus 1 tablespoon caster/granulated sugar**
**300 g/2 sticks plus 4½ tablespoons butter, softened**
**4 ripe bananas**
**freshly squeezed juice of 1 lemon**
**120 g/⅔ cup plus 1 tablespoon dried polenta**
**115 g/½ cup dark soft brown sugar**
**3 large eggs**
**120 g/1 cup shelled pecans, finely ground**
**1 teaspoon vanilla extract**
**1 generous teaspoon ground cinnamon**

***For the rum cream***
**300 ml/1¼ cups double/heavy cream**
**1 generous tablespoon icing/confectioner's sugar, sifted**
**60 ml/¼ cup coconut rum**

*a 25-cm/10-in cast-iron tarte tatin pan or springform cake tin/pan*

Serves 8–10

To prepare the caramel, put 100 g/½ cup of the caster/granulated sugar and 75 g/5 tablespoons of the butter in the tarte tatin pan and warm over direct heat, until the caramel turns golden brown. If using a springform tin/pan melt the sugar and butter in a saucepan until golden brown, then pour the caramel into the prepared pan. Peel the bananas and cut the bananas into 1 cm/½ in rounds and carefully place in rings in the warm caramel. Squeeze over the lemon juice to prevent the bananas from discolouring. Set aside whilst you prepare the polenta cake.

Preheat the oven to 180°C (350°F) Gas 4. Simmer the polenta in the 500 ml/2 cups water for about 5 minutes, until thick then leave to cool. Put the remaining butter and caster/granulated sugar and brown sugar in a mixing bowl and whisk until light and creamy. Beat in the eggs and whisk again. Add the ground pecans, cooked polenta, vanilla extract and cinnamon and whisk together well. Pour the cake batter over the bananas in caramel and bake in the preheated oven for about 1 hour, until the cake is set. If the cake starts to brown too much, cover loosely with a sheet of foil. Let cool in the pan for a few minutes, then invert the cake onto a plate so that the caramelized bananas are on the top. Take care as warm caramel may spill.

To make the rum cream, put the cream, icing/confectioners' sugar and rum in a mixing bowl and whisk to soft peaks. Serve the cake warm with spoonfuls of the rum cream on the side.

This cake will keep for up to 2 days if stored in an airtight container.

# index